THE ART OF MEANINGFUL LIVING

Nov 13th, 2013

Refuse to Struggle.

x - Tal x

THE ART OF MEANINGFUL LIVING

Christopher F. Brown, LCSW, MBA

Art by John Palmer

Synergy Books

The Art of Meaningful Living
Published by Synergy Books
PO Box 80107
Austin, TX 78758

For more information about our books, please write to us, call 512.478.2028, or visit our website at www.synergybooks.net.

Publisher's Cataloging-in-Publication
(Provided by Quality Books, Inc.)

    Brown, Christopher F. (Christopher Frier)
      The art of meaningful living / Christopher F. Brown ;
    [illustrated by John Palmer].
      p. cm.
      LCCN 2008911357
      ISBN-13: 978-0-9821601-7-6
      ISBN-10: 0-9821601-7-8

      1. Self-actualization (Psychology) 2. Success--
    Psychological aspects. 3. Conduct of life. 4. Art,
    Abstract.   I. Palmer, John, 1974- II. Title.

    BF637.S4B819 2009   158.1
                   QBI08-200019

Art reprinted with the permission of John Palmer.

10 9 8 7 6 5 4 3 2 1

"Meaningful living is choosing your passions over your fears. It is accepting what you cannot control and focusing on what is in your power."

To Melissa—for everything you know, and more than I can express. With you, each moment is the best time of my life.

—Christopher

Portrait of Ryan Lindsey, 2004

CONTENTS

Untitled

Bring your focus to it and hold it gently

Collaborators' Note

Thank you for reading *The Art of Meaningful Living*. The abstract art within these pages illustrates concepts that are accepted by clinical professionals in the mental health professions. John Palmer and I decided to combine the worlds of psychology and art because living meaningfully is both a science and an art. Science attempts both to understand and to explain how our world works. Art communicates universally and is interpreted personally. We hope *The Art of Meaningful Living* will be similar. The words address your rational side, while the images appeal to your emotional side. In the same way, meaningful living requires both methodical and creative approaches.

The Art of Meaningful Living can be used in different ways. Use your own imagination to find how its words and images work best for you. The sections are organized in stages; however, the content is fluid. Read the pages from front to back, back to front, or skip around—it's up to you. You can read the book from cover to cover to obtain the cohesive narrative or open to a random page and receive helpful information from that specific reading.

When you want more information on a particular concept, look for the italicized references listed in parentheses.

These will direct you to where you can find detailed information on any specific topic. Also, as we go through *The Art of Meaningful Living*, we will ask you to reflect on certain ideas. These reflections can help you examine how the concepts might apply to your own life. Use any image inside the book as a focal point for building your mindfulness in the present moment (see *Be now*, page 68).

You may find the art beautiful, surprising, and provocative. Adapt *The Art of Meaningful Living* according to your personal style. Some things in these pages will be a fit for you and others will not. Just as the feelings that art evokes are personal and subjective, so too are the key elements of each person's meaningful life. Take what is helpful and leave what is not. The result will be your meaningful life, which is as unique as you are.

> *Adapt* The Art of Meaningful Living *according to your personal style…The result will be your meaningful life, which is as unique as you are.*

Your meaningful life is beautiful. It is strong. It is unique. It is within you. It's fine if it's dormant for now. Together, we will revive it. Your meaningful life is what you are passionate about. Meaningful living requires you to actively choose your behaviors based on your personal elements of meaningful living.

Are you living your meaningful life, or is it buried under hundreds of different disappointments and lost dreams? Unmanaged, your own mind can conceal your meaningful life with dozens of thoughts: "I have to," "I should," "I ought to," and "I should not have" (see *Manage your mind or it will manage you*, page 22).

We are committed to helping you discover your meaningful life. We want to help you see beyond the pain and suffering in your present life to something more powerful and joyful. *The Art of Meaningful Living* is designed to appeal to you on different levels because we all have many different levels of experience.

The book's cover engages your sense of sight. The words address your rational nature, and the abstract depictions of psychological concepts speak to your emotional nature. Be open to your experiences. You do not have to like all of the art or all of the words to get something out of this book. You simply have to understand your own responses.

By understanding your reactions to these stimuli, you can illuminate your passions. We hope that *The Art of Meaningful Living* sparks your passion to sing your song while you still have the precious resource of time.

Thank you for having the courage to consider change.

Please note that significant descriptive details have been intentionally changed when clients are mentioned in order to protect their confidentiality.

You can only be where you are right now

START

Start the art of meaningful living with hope and commitment. Hope is the emotion that says your life can be something valuable. Commitment is accepting that the art of meaningful living requires time, energy, effort, and taking responsibility for all of it.

Hope is essential

Hope

The Art of Meaningful Living is about change, but change is impossible without hope. Meaningful living is choosing your passions over your fears. It is accepting what you cannot control and focusing on what is within your power. Meaningful living is intentional, effective, and respectful. Meaningful lives are built decision by decision, one day at a time. Your meaningful life is unique, as are you. You define your passions and can live them. You can master your mind. You can act in ways that you value. You can have your meaningful life.

> *Meaningful living is choosing your passions over your fears. It is accepting what you cannot control and focusing on what is within your power. Meaningful living is intentional, effective, and respectful.*

If committing to an entire life change is too much for you in this present moment, that's okay. Start your change process where you are right now by finding a small step that you can take toward the life you truly want. Would you like to be able to hope that you can live a meaningful life? The desire to hope is all you need to have in order to start. Acknowledging that meaningful living is possible is the beginning of the journey.

This book offers a way out of desperation. Human desperation can be loud or it can be quiet. People will literally scream in pain when their desperation is excruciating, and those living in shattering desperation can hurt themselves and the people they love in ways that evoke tremendous guilt and sorrow. Do you ever just want to scream? Maybe you feel numb inside, thinking, "Life is not supposed to be like this." Quiet desperation is activity without passion. You get to work on time, handle the in-box, the voice mails, the staff meeting, the annoying co-worker, and your third boss in two years, but there is no passion for any of it. You get up with the kids, fix their breakfast, get them to school, straighten the house, and go to their soccer practice and piano lessons, but you have no personal fulfillment.

There is an illusion that those who are high functioning are successful, happy, and together, but functioning alone does not equate automatically to a meaningful life. There can be a sense of quiet desperation, a feeling that this is not how things are supposed to be. Where did the excitement and passion go? In quiet desperation, we do not seek help from friends, family, or

mental health professionals. Desperate living, whether loudly or quietly, is the opposite of meaningful living. The art of meaningful living combines the everyday functioning of life with personal fulfillment and passion.

With small and progressive adjustments in your daily choices, life can be more than merely going through themotions. When we feel depressed, distressed, bored, or resigned, the idea of filling present moments with meaning seems impossible. It's not. Things can be different. Life will always present you with challenges and obstructions. Some will trigger deep psychological wounds. Meaningful living coexists within our personal journeys of development and psychological healing.

Hope, take a step toward your meaningful life, and turn the page.

Buried under hundreds of different disappointments

Facilitating changes

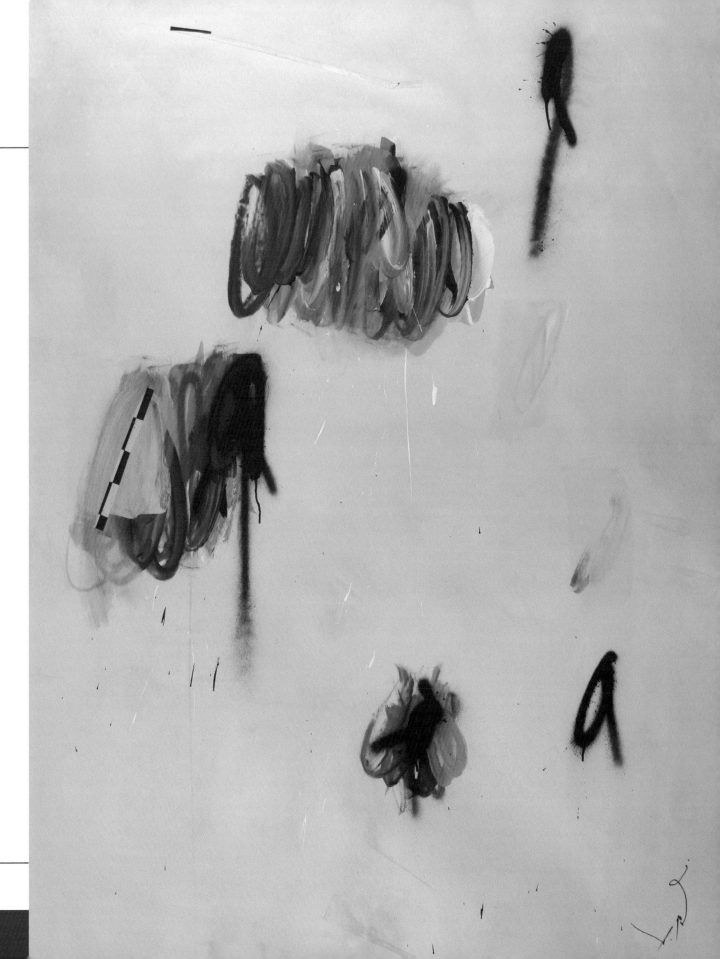

We each have a personal cast of characters in our minds that are based on our experiences of the people we have known. Listen for the voices of your cast that echo within you. "Hearing" your cast doesn't mean that you have schizophrenia. Realize that we can internalize our experiences of other people and keep them with us throughout our lives. Our casts grow as we grow and age. Even those who are lost to us in life remain active within our cast of characters.

The cast can be amazingly helpful, although sometimes they can get in your way. When do certain characters appear in your mind? When do others disappear? What do they say to you? A client of mine hears "Dad" when he makes even the smallest mistake. "Mom's" voice reassures me during difficult times. Listen for the patterns of your cast. Different characters represent voices of authority, reassurance, pride, and fear. They are a gateway to our emotional repertoire. Know your cast, and you begin to know your mind.

I carry each of you in my heart

Acknowledge your cast

Know your cast, and you begin to know your mind.

Let's take a look at your own cast in this exercise called "acknowledgments." Take three minutes of uninterrupted time to make a list of the names that come to your mind when you consider this question: Who do you acknowledge for your being where you are in life now?

Review your list. This is your cast. You will carry them with you all the days of your life.

As I wrote *The Art of Meaningful Living,* I did the exercises too. Here is my cast: Melissa Martinez, Natalee F. Farasey, Herman R. Brown, Kimberly Noble, John K. Hill, Robert Chase Jones, Mark Brown, Louisiana Augustine, H. Hunter Huckabay, Peter Curry, Cabell Tutwiler, Bill Bryan, Christina Lagios Antaky, Connie Amesquita, Roy Case, Vicki Simmons, Michelle Morton McLemore, Linda Boss, Buddy Rhodes, Robert Beck, Aahba Davè, Glen O. Gabbard, John Palmer, Karen Winston, Carol Gilbert, Ellen Gittess, Sharron Mapel, Norma Clarke, John Hart, Sarah Aderholt, Tanya Bennett, Rion Hart, Stewart Twemlow, Chris Marraudino, Amanda Lewis, Jake and Brandy Brown, and all of my clients. To each of you, I say thank you for the lessons you have taught me. I carry each of you in my heart.

Thoughts can be monologues, dialogues, or full cast conversations

Questions to help you discover your cast:

- Where did you grow up, and how did your family come to live there?
- Who raised you?
- Who are your siblings and family members?
- Who did you want to be like when you grew up?
- Where did you go to school?
- Who were your friends and teachers?
- Who were your mentors and coaches?
- Who gave you your first job?
- What do you do for a living, and how did you choose it?
- What do you believe in, and who taught it to you?
- What and who attracts you?
- What repulses you?
- Who are your friends, lovers, enemies, or rivals?
- What are the major milestones in your life, and who was involved in them?

COMMIT

Your life will not change without you facilitating changes. My goal is for you to change from enduring your existence to living with purpose, direction, and meaning. *The Art of Meaningful Living* gives you a basic framework to build a life of passion by developing specific skills and using certain techniques. Learn to build wisdom, take action, and develop resilience. Learn to manage your mind, cope with the world around you, define what is valuable to you, and move toward the life you want. In reading this book, you are on your way.

I strive to make every day stand for something meaningful to me, but simply telling you to do what I do will not work for you. It's your meaningful life we're building, so these ideas must become uniquely yours. Make this framework personal. Be wary of people who tell you they have everything figured out for you, because every person is wonderfully unique. I may enjoy things that you find boring, and you will experience life in

Will you collaborate?
John Palmer and Chris Silkwood

ways that I will never exactly share (see *Stop being right, and start understanding,* page 42). Therefore, your meaningful life by definition will be different from mine, and the plan to build it, if it is to be effective, must be tailored to your values and interests.

Be wary of people who tell you they have everything figured out for you, because every person is wonderfully unique.

This book will give you the information you need. Make it your own. Bend it, break it down, and take what works for you. What do you say? Will you collaborate with me to create your unique, meaningful life?

Committed to those first few steps

WISDOM

There are concepts you must understand before you can effectively build your meaningful life. Wisdom is your accumulated life knowledge. It is gained from the insights of other people and personal experience. The following ideas will get you ready for later action, like aiming before you fire. Mastering the concepts that work for you will help you reach meaningful living faster than if you had to learn each one solely from your own experience.

Solely from your own experience

CHOOSE YOUR STYLE OF LIVING

There are two styles of living: meaningful and avoidant. Each day, we choose one or the other.

When you face a difficult decision, choosing that which you are passionate about, despite the cost, is meaningful living. Conversely, choices that sacrifice zeal to steer clear of pain are what we call avoidant living. By the way, you cannot truly avoid all physical and psychological pain: both are part of life. However, you can learn how to manage either (see *Suffering is human*, page 12).

Avoidant and meaningful choices are mutually exclusive. While you cannot control everything (see *Understand the control problem*, page 18), you can choose your style of living. We usually make this choice passively, but from this moment on, make it consciously. Stop being pushed around by your legacy of hardwired instincts and comfort zones (see *Manage your mind or it will manage you*, page 22).

Avoidant living is like going on a road trip with the goal of never hitting a pothole

While you cannot control everything, you can choose your style of living.

Avoidant living is like going on a road trip with the goal of never hitting a pothole. The best way to achieve that objective is to never leave the house. You'll meet your goal, but you'll never go anywhere. The goal of meaningful living is to reach a destination that you select. You will have obstacles, but you can manage them. If you have a flat tire, you can change it. When you get lost, you can ask for directions and get back on course. Moving toward your dreams is living a meaningful life, but simply trying not to get hurt is living an avoidant one. Avoidant living is a path to quiet desperation.

Clear your mind, and consider this question: Are you living an avoidant life or a meaningful one?

People living in quiet desperation are masterful minimizers

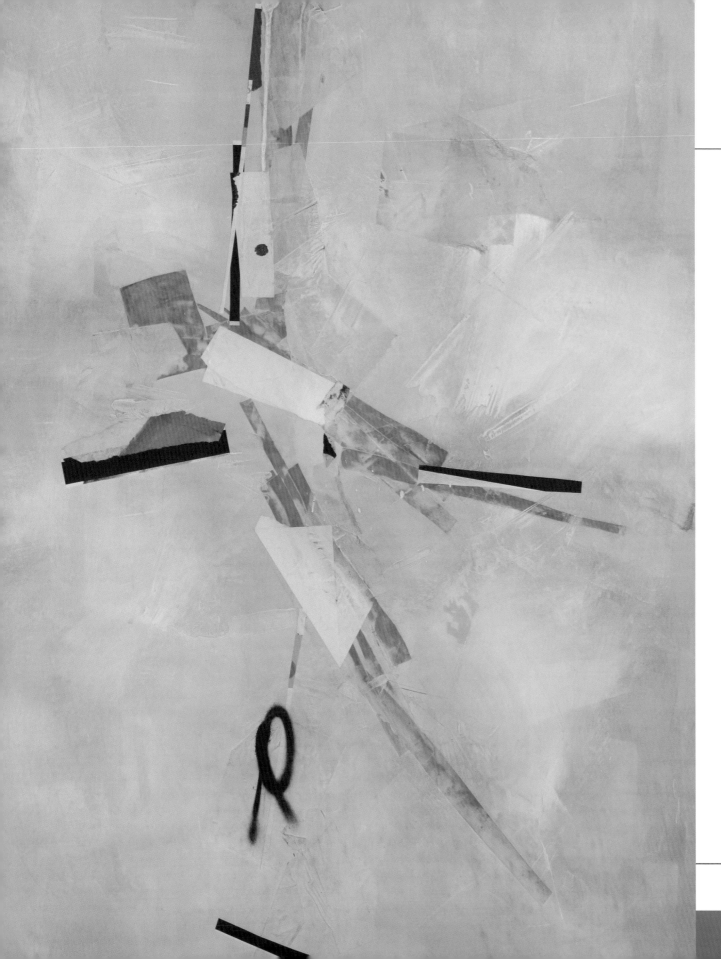

Life is not easy!
—Sigmund Freud, *New Introductory Lectures on Psychoanalysis*

We will all suffer physical and psychological pain; mortality guarantees it. Some of our suffering is inevitable, and some is self-inflicted. Sadly, if you are fortunate enough to live a long life, you will lose loved ones, physical abilities, and possessions. Psychologist Steven Hayes, PhD, suggests in his Relational Frame Theory (RFT) that much of human suffering is a by-product of having the most sophisticated organic brain on the planet. Regardless of the cause, there is no doubt that we suffer more than any other creatures. In his book *Get Out of Your Mind and Into Your Life*, Hayes cites a 2004 research study by John A. Chiles, PhD, and Kirk D. Strosahl, PhD, that found nearly every human being thinks about suicide at some point in his or her life. Suffering can come in the forms of diagnosable mental disorders, marital problems, or chronic pain disorders. Pain is inevitable over the course of a human life. The goal of the avoidant life is to keep away from pain, but that is impossible because suffering is part of the human experience (see *Choose your style of living*, page 10).

Suffering is inevitable and some is self-inflicted

SUFFERING IS HUMAN

The goal of the avoidant life is to keep away from pain, but that is impossible because suffering is part of the human experience.

Why change, if suffering is inevitable? First, you can reduce the pain in your life by minimizing that which is self-inflicted. Second, you can accept life's inevitable suffering in the service of something meaningful: your passions. Self-inflicted suffering is psychological pain generated from within our minds. For example, you might believe that something is wrong with you. Tragically, this kind of belief is all too common. When your mind is convinced that you are defective, it seems like other people have it all. Your mind subjectively evaluates you as bad and all others as good. Your mind says, "I am miserable, and they are happy. I am alone, and they are in love. I hate my job, and they love their careers. They have everything I want." It seems as if you could have that "perfect life" if you could only get rid of your perceived defect. This is self-inflicted psychological suffering. Sound familiar? If so, you are not alone (see *Manage your mind or it will manage you*, page 22).

Minimizing contributes to self-infected suffering. People living in quiet desperation are masterful "minimizers" who believe that their emotional pain somehow does not count because someone else has it worse than them. This is a common strategy for managing psychological suffering, and it is ineffective. Minimizing eventually increases the overall level of emotional pain.

Imagine that you broke your arm in an accident. Minimizing the pain and continuing to use your broken arm would cause greater damage. Furthermore, learning of someone who has a broken arm *and* a broken leg does not mean you should ignore your injury. Your pain is not trivial in the face of others' sufferings. You are hurt and need attention, even if someone else has a severer injury. Perhaps you are grateful that your leg is not broken too, but your pain is real, and you deserve help. Invalidating your own pain can amplify your psychological suffering by adding feelings of guilt and shame. Of course, someone else has it worse than you, but there is no absolute scale to measure relative pain. Each person in the world has his or her emotional and physical pain.

Pain is a form of communication between the body and the mind. Minimize it and you may miss the valid messages sent by your body. Remember that there

are dangerous things in the world that we all must be aware of for our own survival. Without pain, we would not survive because we would not learn to avoid actual harm. The difficulty lies in determining legitimate threats from imagined ones (see *Manage your mind or it will manage you*, page 22). Having pain does not mean that you are "weak" or "bad." This core belief is a poor foundation on which to build your meaningful life. The key is the relationship between you and your pain. View pain as information, reflect upon it, and make considered choices (see *Reflect on your mind*, page 24). If you are a minimizer, it's time to find a new strategy.

Although tragedies will happen in your life, they will not destroy you. While you will feel emotional and physical pain, suffering doesn't have to define your life. Suffering defines an avoidant life. Meaningful living requires the acceptance of suffering from circumstances beyond your control. Suffering simply means that you're human, so suffer in service of your passions (see *Define your passions*, page 52).

BUILD AWARENESS

What is necessary to change a person is to change his awareness of himself.
—Abraham Maslow, *Religions, Values, and Peak Experiences*

From the outside, my client, Paul, seemed like the life of the party. He made friends everywhere he went with his quirky sense of humor and good nature. While not at the top of his high school class, he made solid grades. He was the youngest of three kids, all born to loving parents married for more than thirty years. He was on the high school football team and enjoyed being outdoors. Despite all of these strengths, as he was about to graduate from high school and head to college out of state, he grew anxious. Eventually, he could not go to school or even leave his house because of his severe distress.

Paul did not suffer from an obvious trauma or loss, and no one in his life was ill or dying. His family could not understand the changes in Paul's behavior, and they became alarmed. Clearly something was happening beyond everyone's awareness. Until Paul could understand what was happening within him, he could not explain it to anyone, and he was powerless to change anything.

Listen to your thoughts for a day

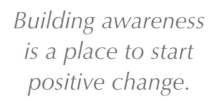

Building awareness is a place to start positive change.

In Paul's situation, and others like it, building awareness is a place to start positive change. Awareness diffuses much of our pain's perceived strength and charts a path out of emotional paralysis. When Paul and I started our work together, he gave me his typical good-natured charm. This was the persona he presented to everyone. Personas are the versions of ourselves that we show to other people—sometimes even those very close to us. Personas are like masks that both protect and obscure the person wearing them. Paul's happy-go-lucky persona attracted people to him, which encouraged him to keep using it. It was the mask to which his family was accustomed, so when he began to struggle, they could not initially understand it.

We all have multiple personas that we cultivate intentionally or adapt unconsciously. You might have one persona at work, another in the community, and a third within your family. Maybe you are the entertainer who can always be counted on to lighten up a tense situation with the right joke or funny comment. You might develop a stylish veneer that appears unflappable and impenetrable to those around you. Maybe you're that white knight always looking for the damsel in distress. Some adopt a sense of naive helplessness that inevitably draws others in to rescue them. I once worked for a salesman who mastered the persona of a lovable but bumbling "good ol' boy" because he made more sales when people felt sorry for him.

We all have a real person under our personas. Do you let people see the real you? Paul didn't—unless you listened carefully. When I really listened to Paul, I began to discover that he was down on himself sometimes. He would drop hints that he didn't think he was very smart or very handsome or very talented. Curious about Paul's habit of beating up on himself and wondering how pervasive it was, I asked him to track the number of times during the day he thought something negative about himself. The next day, he told me he had stopped counting at fifty—and that was in the first three hours! He had never been aware of how much he beat up on himself. Until he built this awareness, he was powerless to interrupt the pattern.

As Paul began to understand the person beneath his persona, he saw that he was insecure and scared. He hid this person from almost everyone, including

Build awareness

his friends and family. He learned that he was understandably nervous about the big change in his life: graduating from high school and going to college. He had to develop awareness of his persona, his negative self-talk, and his stress about going to college before he could overcome his anxiety.

*Do not judge
yourself too harshly*

Like Paul, are you too hard on yourself? Listen to your thoughts for a day. Try not to believe every thought. Just have them and notice if any patterns emerge. It is important to notice if you beat yourself up with your thoughts. "I'm not good enough." "No one will ever love me." "I'm too fat." "I'll never be successful." "I'm lazy." "I'm a loser." "I hate my legs." "There's no way I could do that." "I'm no good." "I'm so stupid." "I'm worthless." Do any of these sound familiar? Consider if your thoughts are legitimate developmental needs or pathological self-criticism and loathing. When you have the habit of beating yourself up, self-critical thoughts stick in your mind like that annoying television jingle; the more you try not to think about it, the more it's there. Imagine hearing that advertisement fifty times a day. That's what happens in the minds of chronic self-critics.

Develop your ability to **notice** your thoughts without automatically believing them. This skill can help you break the cycle of negative self-talk. Don't try to stop thoughts from occurring. Remember, that will only make the thoughts occur more frequently (see *Understand the control problem*, page 18). Instead, just notice when you beat yourself up. Observe how many times a day your mind slugs you with condemnation, criticism, and general meanness. After you notice the negative self-talk, **assign new meaning** with another thought. You could say to yourself, "there goes a neuron firing in my brain," "there's that pattern starting again," or "my mind is telling me that I'm a loser." Hayes is fond of thanking his mind for any thought he has because it is evidence that he has a superior brain that is capable of thought.

If you notice negative thoughts in your mind, try to be more kind to yourself. Ask yourself, "Would I say this to my best friend?" Not a chance! Be your own best friend. Kids need to hear about seven compliments for each criticism they receive in order to maintain healthy self-esteem. Apply the same rule to yourself as an adult. I know plenty of people who criticize themselves fifty times a day but very few who respond with three hundred fifty compliments. By the way, those three hundred fifty compliments are needed just to stay psychologically healthy. Building a healthy self-esteem requires more than that. How many negative things are you saying to yourself each day? How many compliments do you give yourself daily?

Build a repertoire of compliments to counter your mind's self-critical thoughts.

Bringing the problem to your awareness

Sit in a comfortable space and, with no distractions, spend five minutes focused on this exercise. Imagine the most supportive person you have known in your life (see *Acknowledge your cast*, page 4). This person might be a parent, a friend, a spouse, or even a therapist. Can you see him or her in your mind? Imagine his or her answers to this question: What are all of the good things about me?

List all the answers. Each time you criticize yourself, imagine this wonderfully supportive person in your mind, and have him or her counter that criticism with eight compliments.

How many good things did you find about yourself in three hundred seconds? Develop fifty compliments for yourself or more. Be honest and revel in your strengths. Celebrate them instead of being embarrassed or uncertain. These are the compliments that you are going to give yourself after you notice your mind beating up on you. Enlist friends, family members, co-workers, and anyone else you can think of to help you develop your list. If you are self-critical, commit these compliments to memory because you are going to be responding with them often.

What patterns are holding you back from your meaningful life?

Once you gain a higher level of awareness of what is happening within and around you, start looking for patterns. Paul's patterns of negative thinking triggered powerful anxiety that threatened to overwhelm him. With help, he broke the negative thinking patterns so he could live the life he wanted as a college student. What patterns are holding you back from your meaningful life? Maybe you struggle with negative thinking, chronic anxiety, or traumatic memories. You could be chronically sick or have urges to isolate yourself from other people. What in your environment triggers your patterns? The answers to these questions can empower you to move toward meaningful living.

Maintain healthy self-esteem

God grant me the serenity to accept the things I cannot change, the courage to change the things I can, and the wisdom to know the difference.
—Anonymous

I hosted a discussion on psychotherapy techniques at a training clinic in Houston, Texas. Over lunch, one doctor talked about a common dilemma. She said, "I know what (my client) needs to do, but I just can't get him to *do* it!"

Focusing your energy on things you cannot control or influence leads to ineffectiveness, disappointment, and frustration.

This is what I call "the control problem." There are things in your life that you can control, others that you can only influence, and even more that you are powerless over. Focus your efforts on what you can control or influence. Here, you have the power to be effective. Effectiveness builds positive self-esteem.

Expecting to control things

Understand the control problem

Conversely, focusing your energy on things you cannot control or influence leads to ineffectiveness, disappointment, and frustration. When you try to change things that are out of your control, it drains you of your energy, leaves you feeling powerless, and generates low self-esteem. It's like trying to drive one hundred miles per hour with your car in second gear. It makes meaningful living impossible.

What do you spend energy on that is out of your control or influence?

The Serenity Prayer, presented at the opening of this section, illustrates three skills central to meaningful living: acceptance, change, and discernment. These same skills have helped millions of people around the world recover from destructive compulsive behaviors like substance abuse, compulsive gambling, overeating, and sex addiction.

Acceptance is an active process. It is not resignation. Resignation implies that you are a victim who must passively endure whatever happens to you. When we accept a situation, we stop spending energy fighting something that is out of our control and take in the full current experience for what it is—no more and no less. In Acceptance and Commitment Therapy (ACT), acceptance is defined as embracing the psychological experience of an event, without unnecessary avoid-ance, while also behaving effectively. Acceptance requires acknowledgment of the limits of our abilities to make things the way we want them. Acceptance does not imply hopelessness. Rather, accepting realities and constraints frees you to focus your power in areas where you have leverage.

Change is the act of making something different, and in this context, it is the ability to make an object or situation into what we want it to be. For example, John Palmer has the ability to convert an empty canvas into the artwork he imagines. He has the power to make that change happen. Similarly, one of my clients, unable to work for years, became suc-cessfully employed after focus-ing his power on eliminating the self-inflicted obstacles that pre-vented him from getting a job. He changed his situation from unem-ployment and dependence to em-ployment and self-reliance. This change helped him build healthy self-esteem. Create changes by following these steps. First, have a clear idea of the outcome you want. Second, develop a strategy to get what you want and implement it. Third, after an adequate amount of time, analyze your progress without bias.

Acceptance is an active process

Discernment is the ability to tell the difference between what you can and cannot control. Often we become so enamored with our strategies that we stick with them even when the results are ineffective and undesired. Recently I spoke with a parent who was trying to get her adult daughter to be sober by coercing her into rehab for the third time. This change effort failed all three times because Mom was effectively discerning. She was trying to control her adult daughter's choices, and other people's behavioral choices are not in our power to control. Analyze the change strategies in your life with the clinical detachment of a scientist, and if you are not getting the result you want, focus on getting results that require only your own energy and efforts to achieve success. For example, my goal while driving on the highway might be to travel safely from where I am to where I want to be. Which strategy is more likely to be effective: getting everyone on the road to drive the way I want them to do or focusing on my own driving? The latter is more effective because I cannot force fellow drivers to do anything, no matter how much energy I dedicate to the effort.

The world is full of things that are out of our control, like the weather, the price of gas, the state of the world economy, and other people, just to name a few.

Do not imagine a pink elephant dancing a ballet in a pink tutu

Spending your time and energy focused on these types of things will likely yield many ineffective results. Conversely, focusing your effort on yourself and your behaviors will be much more successful for you. Prepare yourself by carrying an umbrella, buying a fuel-efficient vehicle, or increasing your personal income. If you are willing, complete the following exercise to illustrate the point.

Make a fist with your right hand. Barring a physical disability, making a fist is within your control. It is a behavior that you can choose to do or not to do. Remember, you have the most power over your own actions. Next, focus on your thoughts. Thoughts are an area where we have influence but not complete control. You cannot stop automatic thoughts from occurring in your mind.

Do not imagine a pink elephant dancing ballet in a tutu.

See what I mean? In fact, when you work very hard at trying not to have certain thoughts, you will have the thoughts more often. You cannot control every thought that occurs to you, but you can give your mind new thoughts. Again, if you are willing, please accept a new thought from me.

Take ten seconds to clear your mind. Once you are clear of distractions, read the following sentence five times: I am capable.

You were not thinking, "I am capable" before you read the sentence, but you are now. As you need to, you can give yourself new thoughts. This is particularly useful if you are prone to negative self-talk or ineffective judgments (see *Stop being right, and start understanding*, page 42). Allow thoughts to flow into your awareness and then out again, rather than trying to stop them from occurring, and give yourself new thoughts as you need them. Remember, you can only influence your thoughts, not control them.

Happiness is not a destination; it is an experience you will have on the way there.

Like thoughts, feelings are impressionable, not controllable. Being "happy" is not as simple as making a fist or thinking "I am capable." "Happy" is not something you can simply do. Feelings are fleeting experiences that follow behaviors and thoughts. In other words, happiness is not a destination; it is an experience you will have on the way there. Your personal passions, or prioritized elements of meaningful living, are more reliable destinations than feelings (see *Define your passions*, page 52).

Skills for managing the control problem:

The **acceptance** skill is the ability to embrace all aspects of an event without avoiding uncomfortable emotional experiences, while also behaving in accordance with the elements of your meaningful life.

The **change** skill is intentionally impacting a situation to create an outcome that we imagine.

The **discernment** skill is the ability to successfully differentiate between areas that you have the power to change and those that you do not.

Mind management

Your most personal computer

Your mind is the most personal of computers. It has hardware and software. The brain, or your mind's hardware, is far more "plastic" than previously thought. Brain imaging technology shows that structural and functional changes in the brain are possible with focused and consistent changes in behaviors over time. Psychotherapy, psychopharmacology, and structured mindfulness exercises are among the things that can literally change your brain.

Your mind comes "loaded" with some software. We are each born with a temperament that is present regardless of our home environments. Easygoing, anxious, cautious, or mixed temperaments are hardwired into our minds. In the same home, one child could be easy to soothe, while another is difficult. Your childhood temperament is still present to some degree in adulthood.

Reflect on your style. If you are reticent in social situations, your temperament might be cautious. Perhaps you are easily hurt emotionally, and it takes you a while to talk yourself into feeling better. This indicates a basic temperament that is difficult to soothe. Maybe things roll off your back with ease. This may indicate that you have an easygoing temperament. Perhaps you see aspects of all three within you. Whatever your temperament,

You are human

you were born with it, and it is okay. In fact, it is perfect. Your temperament is part of what makes you unique and special.

Other software, like how we connect to others and how we see the world and ourselves, gets programmed into our minds as we develop during the course of our lives. The first "programmers" of our personalities are the important adults from our childhoods. They teach us about life explicitly but also implicitly. For example, boys learn to be a man, in part, by watching the men around them. Likewise, women model adulthood for young girls. Our parents format our personalities with a basic model of how relationships work. You can think of this as your personality 1.0. New versions are created as you grow up, by life experience and new relationships. They give you the opportunity to challenge old assumptions and programs; however, the shadows of old programs remain (see *Listen for your mind's programming*, page 86).

Manage your mind or it will manage you

Living creatures react to experience; this stimulus and response interaction is fundamental to psychology. Human minds, however, are special. We live with two realities: one around us, another within us. Human beings respond to external experiences as well as internal ones, like thoughts and feelings. Our complex world triggers the mind constantly. Responses themselves become new stimuli, resulting in second-order responses, and they can quickly build like a giant snowball. Acting on your every instinct is like giving up your free will.

News headlines display examples daily. A recent story read, "Police: Man opens gift early; wife stabs him." Clearly, this woman did not reflect on all of her options before she grabbed that kitchen knife. This is an extreme, though relevant, example. However, these types of disproportionate reactions can happen in the most mundane, everyday circumstances. Meaningful living requires that you resist these kinds of impulsive responses. You do not have to be hijacked by your instincts. Instead, you can manage your mind.

You are not your mind. Your mind is a functionary. It serves a purpose like your hands or feet. By managing your mind, you can experience a stimulus, observe your mind's internal reactions, mull over your possible responses, reflect on your knowledge from past experiences, and choose a considered action.

You are not your mind

Pause and reflect are two important mind management skills. They prevent our minds from being hijacked by our natural impulses. **Pause** buys you time to collect your thoughts and feelings before choosing your action. To use the pause skill, imagine that a digital video recorder is monitoring you, and you have the remote control. You can press your internal pause button as soon as you know that you are emotionally triggered. **Reflect** requires you to be curious rather than overly judgmental (see *Stop being* right, *and start understanding,* page 42). Assume that all behavior has a purpose and its nature is not always obvious. Be curious about why you do the things you

do. Presume that you are trying to solve a problem with every behavior. Reflect on what problems you are trying to solve. Ask yourself if your strategies are effective, and consider all of the consequences of every strategy.

Reflect on this: we are capable of multiple reactions in a world full of complex interactions. However, our options narrow when our level of emotions peaks. This is our biological response to stress commonly known as "fight or flight." The pause skill allows us to expand our options in the face of stress. Using your reflection skill allows you to make purposeful choices as you move toward meaningful living.

> *You cannot control the thoughts and feelings you have, but you can choose their meanings.*

You cannot control the thoughts and feelings you have, but you can choose their meanings. Misinterpreting them can lead to more avoidance and self-inflicted suffering. For example, anxiety typically means "danger." Your heart rate goes up, adrenaline releases, and your eyes dilate slightly with this interpretation. These are all appropriate responses when your life is at risk, but not when you have to give

a speech in public or in the middle of a benign family outing.

What are some of the thoughts and feelings that trouble you most? Can you assign new meanings to those experiences? Could nervousness and anxiety be growing pains that are actually signs of "growth" instead of "danger"? This is similar to giving yourself a new thought. Use your observation skills to consider your thoughts and feelings carefully as they happen. Imagine that you are window-shopping: you can choose if you want to just look at those thoughts and feelings or buy them. To illustrate, imagine an issue that you are struggling with currently. After you have a topic in mind, clear your mind of distraction, focus on the issue, and observe your full range of thoughts and feelings for five minutes. If your mind continually returns to a particular idea or emotion, after five minutes, focus on that.

What new meanings can you assign to troubling thoughts and feelings?

Reflect on your mind

The mind is like an iceberg, it floats with one-seventh of its bulk above water.
—Sigmund Freud

Pioneer psychiatrist Sigmund Freud named three layers of the human mind as the conscious, preconscious, and unconscious. Consciousness includes the thoughts and feelings that run through your mind at any present moment. Consciousness is the tip of the iceberg. Preconscious material can enter your awareness with a cue. For example, what is your cell phone number? That question cued you to recall the number when you were not thinking it previously. The unconscious contains material beyond your awareness that, nonetheless, drives your thoughts, feelings, and behavior. Hold Freud's concept of the multilayered mind in your consciousness while you reflect on another.

> *The unconscious contains material beyond your awareness that, nonetheless, drives your thoughts, feelings, and behavior.*

Psychologist Marsha Linehan, PhD, describes our minds as having emotional and rational sides that overlap. You reason and problem solve with your rational mind. Making a budget, writing a report, and fixing a leaky faucet are rational mind functions. Your emotional mind is comprised of your feelings and intuition. Falling in love, sensing danger, and following your passions are all emotional mind tasks. Do you typically lead with your head or heart? The key to good decisions is engaging both

Prioritized elements of meaningful living

sides of your mind. According to Linehan, this is your "wise mind." When you think that something is right and feels right, that is generally a wise mind decision.

Use the **wise mind** skill by focusing your mind on a particular question. Notice your breathing. Ask yourself a question as you inhale; then, as you exhale, listen for the answer. It's okay if the answer doesn't come to you immediately. Your mind simply needs more time to process the question on all three levels: conscious, preconscious, and unconscious.

Modern culture predominately trains and rewards our rational minds. When was the last time that you saw a bumper sticker reading "My Kid is an Emotionally Self-aware Student at Central High School"? It is all too common for people to have an overdeveloped rational side and a neglected emotional side. Sometimes, people with finely tuned emotional minds get labeled as "overly sensitive," "too emotional," or "thin-skinned." If you have ever been told this, you have been done a tremendous disservice. Emotions are not bad. Feelings do not make you weak. Quite the contrary, emotions are critical to effective decision making. They are your sixth sense. If you have been told through the years that you "should use your head (rational side) instead of your heart (emotional side)," you have been told to make decisions with only half of your mind. In the context of meaningful

Observation skills

living, it is mandatory that you use both your rational and emotional minds.

Know the products of your mind

Mind monitoring is listening for the five "products" of your mind: thoughts, feelings, memories, sensations, and urges, then successfully interpreting the information each gives you. Immediately judging the products of your mind as good or bad diffuses the complexity of those products. They are all unique, multilayered, and informative. However, your mind gives you information that, upon reflection, may or may not be valid.

Thoughts are the most well-known product of our minds. Thoughts can come from our rational and emotional sides. Even when we sleep, we are thinking in our dreams. Thoughts come to our minds in all different forms. Thoughts can be like lines of text or spoken words. They can occur as images and pictures. Thoughts can be monologues, dialogues, or full cast conversations (see *Acknowledge your cast*, page 4). However your thoughts come to you is okay. The important thing is to be aware of them.

When monitoring, consider that many thoughts are invalid. Invalid thoughts can originate in your childhood experiences. Things that were valid in your family of origin may no longer fit in your adulthood.

Thoughts

Feelings Triptych

Invalid thoughts can originate from prolonged depression or anxiety states. Regardless of cause, believing invalid thoughts leads to serious problems in living. You move away from your meaningful life by acting on old, distorted, ineffective thoughts. Thinking something does not make it true. Hayes says, "Thoughts are thoughts; thoughts aren't facts."

What thoughts are you treating like facts in your life?

Feelings are a vital product of your mind. Strengthen your emotional mind by building an emotional vocabulary. Researchers Paul Ekman, PhD, and Wallace Friesen, PhD, identified six core emotions present in infants: happiness, surprise, fear, disgust, sadness, and anger. Consider core emotions as "feeling families." Each core emotion is comprised of many feelings that represent varying degrees of intensity. The happiness feeling family contains

the intense, such as joy and bliss; the moderate, such as gladness; and the mild, such as amused, entertained, and pleased. The anger family starts with annoyance and irritation and ends with rage and hatred. Watch daytime television to build your emotional vocabulary. Soap operas and talk shows vividly display intense emotions for their audiences. Name the emotions that you see coming from the people on the television screen. Then imagine when you might have had feelings similar to those you see on the screen.

Reflect on your emotions, or your sixth sense, as these messages are vital to your physical and mental health. The ability to describe and discuss feelings is so vital to mental health that the lack of it is a clinical disorder called alexithymia. The inability to label and discuss feelings may force you to act them out. For example, unidentified or unresolved grief may lead to depression, isolation, and withdrawal from life. Unarticulated anxiety or desperation can lead to compulsive drinking, spending, or sex. If you cannot hear what your feelings are saying, your emotional mind remains underdeveloped, often resulting in self-destructive behavior.

> *If you cannot hear what your feelings are saying, your emotional mind remains underdeveloped, often resulting in self-destructive behavior.*

Thanks to your complex mind, you can experience many feelings simultaneously. You could be happy and surprised, excited and scared, hopeful and concerned—all in the exact same moment. You can have opposite feelings simultaneously. Many of my clients love and hate their parents simultaneously. This leads to confusion, a third simultaneous emotional experience.

The opposite of alexithymia is emotional dysregulation, or flooding, where you are overwhelmed with emotions to the point that your functioning is impaired. When guilt, anxiety, sadness, and anger seem overwhelming, the rational mind is constrained, and you cannot make considered choices. My client, Bill, was so angry after a negative performance review that he impulsively quit his job on the spot. He did not have another job lined up, had no other source of income, and had a mortgage to pay. In session, we were able to see how the intensity of his anger drove him to sabotage himself. Had he been able to pause, reflect, and engage his whole mind in the decision-making process, he might have planned his exit in a thoughtful way that would have been easier on himself and his family.

If you become so intensely emotional that you temporarily lose rationality, analyze your pattern. Learn the signposts down the road

Feelings
_____

to flooding. Maybe you become easily tearful, argue more often, have sleep problems, or eat a dozen chocolate chip cookies in one sitting (like me). Once you build awareness, employ effective strategies to soothe your emotional mind so that you can reengage your rational mind. Distract from intense feelings by reading, watching

a movie, or talking to someone else about their life. Physical exercise can combat flooding. You can burn away intense feeling levels as if they were calories. The goal is not to eliminate your feeling but to stop the flooding so that you can feel and think your way through the situation. Discussing your feelings can also help you regulate emotions, but talking about your feelings when you are flooded can be a stimulus for more emotional responses. When you are flooded with intense feeling, distract first and discuss your feelings when they are less intense.

Flooding is more likely when your stress level is high, so set boundaries when your emotions are escalating. Boundaries are like fences that keep valuable things in and unwanted things out. Good boundaries reduce the stimuli in the environment that might trigger more emotional responses. For example, after a heated argument, a knock on the door or a ringing cell phone might ignite an eruption of anger unintentionally. Set boundaries by closing the door or turning off the cell phone until your emotions return to a manageable level. Focusing on the experience of your feelings is the opposite of distraction, and if you do it skillfully, it can help prevent flooding (see *Have all of your experiences*, page 70).

Process intense feelings by reviewing them with another person. Successful processing includes discussion and validation. Having your emotions acknowledged and

Memories

normalized as part of the human experience reduces psychological pain. Psychotherapy is a safe place for processing. A trained professional with whom you have an established relationship can help you work through feelings without inadvertently triggering more flooding.

Before we move on to the next product of your mind, let's consider happiness. Many people I meet have the life goal to "be happy." This is an unreliable goal. Happiness, like all emotions, is ephemeral. Some say that the experience of a single emotion lasts fifteen seconds. Other studies show that feelings will dissipate in about ninety minutes without a new trigger. For better and worse, feelings do not last. Your personal passions are more reliable destinations for your life's journey, and happiness will be a recurring experience along the way. Having meaning and value in your life is the goal, whereas positive emotions are the by-product of consistently working toward your passions. You will no longer be controlled by negative feelings because you can act according to your passions, regardless of how you feel in a given moment.

Memories are the next product of the mind. They are past experiences that are stored in our minds in the form of thoughts with feelings attached. Some memories can be so painful that they get in the way of your meaningful life. Sarah's memories of past trauma arose from her mind at

Sensations

random times, and her body responded as if she were being victimized all over again. The resulting anxiety was debilitating. We worked together to redefine her memories by using the skill of assigning meaning. We decided to add a thought to Sarah's mind when her traumatic memories arose. The new thought was, "this memory is only a series of neurons firing in my brain." Next, she learned to connect with her experience in the present moment (see *Be now*, page 68). She then gave herself more new thoughts to remind her that she was not suffering the traumas all over again. With the notice skill, she observed her total experience as it occurred in her body and mind. By challenging the automatic meanings assigned by her mind, accurately labeling her experiences, and actively managing the present moment, Sarah can have these memories without living an avoidant life. At the end of our work together, she said, "It's not so bad really. I have all of these traumatic memories, but that means that I also have memories of the wonderful things that have happened to me. There are a lot more good than bad." Traumatic memories are very serious and, if unchecked, can cause adverse consequences. But you can have a meaningful life along with any traumatic experiences.

The human mind-body connection allows you to get information from your emotional mind through physiological

Urges

sensations, another product of the mind. My client, James, experienced his feelings through his stomach. To check how he felt, he listened to his belly. The belly knew when he was contented, nervous, confident, or upset. Each emotional experience brought a different physiological response. We built an emotional vocabulary for the feelings that each of these sensations represented. Under stress, some people clench their jaws, experience muscle tightness, or unconsciously make fists with their hands. Where in your body do you experience emotions?

> *Your mind produces an urge in order to deliver a message, and decoding that message allows you to deal with the triggering event successfully.*

The final product of the mind is behavioral **urges**, such as impulses to scratch an itch, take a drink, and wash your hands. As with all the products of the mind, the trigger for behavioral urges can come either from your external environment or within yourself. You may have the same urge to flinch and pull into yourself in response to either a loud noise or a sudden jolt of fear. Sufferers of obsessive compulsive disorder (OCD) have great difficulty resisting urges that are triggered by unwanted, intrusive thoughts. While

you may not suffer from OCD, some urges can still be difficult to resist. Remember that urges are not good or bad. Instead, think of urges as conditioned responses. They just are. Your mind produces an urge in order to deliver a message, and decoding that message allows you to deal with the triggering event successfully. Use your mind monitoring skills to observe urges. Reflect on what a particular urge means to you. Assign new meanings to urges as needed, and act thoughtfully to channel them in a productive manner.

Tuning in to your mind is complex and multifaceted. Initially, it may seem daunting to monitor your thoughts, feelings, sensations, memories, and behavioral urges and then decode all that information so you can act in a way that fits your personal passions. But you can do it. Over time, you will master these skills and use them automatically (see *Learn the learning curve*, page 48). Once you develop your expert skill in mind management, you will stop constantly reacting to your mind and instead act in a thoughtful, intentional manner. Choosing your actions, instead of impulsively reacting, is movement toward meaningful living. Remember, however, that no one responds perfectly to every situation. We are human. With hindsight, there will always be things that you would do differently. Keep a curious and reflective stance, don't beat yourself up, learn from your mistakes, and do something different next time (see *Make new mistakes*, page 96).

Mind Management Skills:

The **notice** skill is the ability to neutrally observe your experiences for just what they are: nothing more and nothing less. You can notice events happening around you and experiences happening within you. The key to effective noticing is the neutrality. Do not editorialize, just observe the facts. Apply the notice skill to the products of your mind (thoughts, feelings, memories, sensations, and urges) so that you can have them without automatically believing them. This skill also helps build awareness of patterns in the products of your mind. The notice skill can also be thought of as mind monitoring or observing your mind.

Once you notice your experiences, the **reflect** skill allows you to develop and consider different meanings for the products of your mind before taking action. Give yourself a range of options. Your first interpretation of events and experiences is one possible explanation, but use the reflect skill to see the situation from multiple points of view. Borrow from your cast. Imagine how Mom, Dad, your partner, therapist, and co-worker would see the experience. What would you tell your best friend if they were in a similar situation? The **assign meaning** skill then allows you to choose what the experience means according to which interpretation works best for you.

The **pause** skill is the ability to stop your behavior as you are having an intense experience, like emotional flooding. Use the pause skill until your mind is under control, and then act.

Using the **wise mind** skill allows you to access both the emotional and rational sides of your mind to make important life decisions. Decisions are made from the wise mind only when your emotional and rational minds agree on a choice together.

We all experience problems in living. These are struggles that reduce the quality of our personal or professional lives. When people learn that I am a psychotherapist, they often ask me if I think they have one mental disorder or another. They ask questions like these: "If I like having a glass of white wine at night, am I an alcoholic?" or "If I check to see if the front door is locked before I leave the house, do I have OCD?" or "I have mood swings—does that mean I'm bipolar?" It is impossible to diagnose a disorder from this small amount of information because we all experience anxiety, sadness, and grief. We all have idiosyncratic aspects of our personalities. It is when these experiences cause dramatic problems in living for significant periods of time that professional evaluation is warranted. Whether your problems in living qualify for a disorder or not, they will not improve until you own them and take responsibility for addressing them.

Abraham Harold Maslow, PhD, defined a hierarchy of life needs for human beings. Understanding it can help you become aware of your problems in living. Starting with the most fundamental, Maslow's hierarchy of life needs is basic biological,

Describing and discussing feelings

OWN YOUR PROBLEMS IN LIVING

personal safety, socialization, personal esteem, and self-actualization. Think of these needs as a sort of staircase. There are problems in living associated with every stairstep, and after you climb one, you face the challenge of the next. The following describes these stairsteps in detailed order.

The first two steps on Maslow's staircase of needs are somewhat uniform for all of us. To thrive, humans must have their biological needs for food, water, sex, and shelter successfully addressed. It's the first step, and you cannot skip it. When your problem in living is not having food to eat, it trumps all other concerns. When we are adequately nourished physically, the second step is safety. Safety includes physical well-being and emotional protection. Emotional protection requires structure and limits. In families, children have less overall anxiety and more security when parents provide rules and consequences for them. In adulthood, people function at a higher level when they have structured responsibilities and accountability to others. The structure provides us safety.

Your unique style and preferences come to the forefront in the third step of social needs. For example, each of us has a combination of extroverted and introverted

A meaningful life along with traumatic experiences

traits. Extroverts get energy from being around other people, while introverts recharge with time alone. Even the most introverted of us needs connections with others. Love and belonging are required for Maslow's vision of life fulfillment. While human beings are not designed to be alone, we each have different degrees of relational needs. Focus on the following question to build awareness of your preference: Do you get more energy from being with others or from having time alone?

Your answer cannot be wrong. It's what is right for you. Knowing your social style

makes it easier for you to make choices that meet your own social needs. Social needs can be met through relationships with family members, friends, intimate partners, communities, and co-workers.

Becoming self-actualized does not inoculate you from physical and emotional pain. You can, however, learn to deal with your pain in ways that protect the life you build.

The next step is healthy self-esteem. When you are struggling with meeting basic biological needs and maintaining security, the pain of low self-esteem holds less immediate significance. However, low self-esteem often leads to lives full of quiet desperation. We gain good, healthy self-esteem from positive recognition, reputation, achievements, and status. Remember that your own needs are as important as the needs of those around you—not more and not less. Do not be completely self-centered, as this will impede your social needs by driving people away from relationships with you. Similarly, being completely neglectful of your needs in relationships will

Impulsively reacting

cause you to be resentful, and prolonged resentment will impede your social needs by driving you away from relationships with other people.

The last step is reaching your full potential, what Maslow called self-actualization. This is your meaningful life actualized. The contents of *The Art of Meaningful Living* are meant to help you move toward your personal peak. Becoming self-actualized does not inoculate you from physical and emotional pain (see *Suffering is human*, page 12). You can, however, learn to deal with your pain in ways that protect the life you build.

Learn what stairstep you are standing on by studying the problems you have. If you are always hungry or thirsty, you are on the first step. Chronic worry about your physical health and security are hallmarks of the second step. Struggles with low self-esteem indicate that you have climbed high on the staircase of needs. Remember to give yourself credit for how far you have come while still striving for more.

Something meaningful

Maslow's Hierarchy of Human Needs:

Basic biological needs
Personal safety and security
Socialization
Personal esteem
Self-actualization

THE CONTROL PROBLEM IS IN YOUR RELATIONSHIPS TOO

Samantha came into my office because her fourth marriage was going down the tubes. She and her husband were sleeping in different rooms, they barely spoke to each other when they were alone, and she couldn't remember the last time they had had sex together. The distance between them was enormous. In fact, she started looking for a therapist after she discovered her partner's numerous affairs.

As Samantha told me her story, we discovered that she often had these kinds of relationship problems. Basically, she would fall madly in love, believing her new partner to be "the greatest man in the world." Soon, they would be living together and financially dependent on each other, then usually, but not always, married. It seemed to happen "before I even knew what was happening," Samantha said. According to the pattern, within a couple of years of living together, the relationships stagnated and ended in flames. Then the whole cycle started again with a new partner.

As we began to understand her pattern, Samantha realized she was attracted to partners who were financially independent and physically attractive but emotionally distant or absent. She expected these people to meet all of her relationship needs, but they were ill-equipped for the job. She became passive once the relationship matured, deferring to her partner on issues from where they lived to the friends they had and what they ate for dinner. Samantha eventually resented the loss of herself, but instead of asserting herself, she pulled away from her partner. The sexual intimacy in her relationships waned with the growing emotional distance. We speculated this drove her partners farther from her. Eventually, these emotionally distant men sought new sexual relationships. Samantha was left feeling understandably hurt and betrayed, and at a loss for how to put her life together again.

It would have been easy to blame Samantha's problems on her "no-good" partners. However, blaming did not help Samantha build awareness of her patterns in long-term relationships or stop the pattern from continuing. Samantha was the common denominator, and once she saw her contribution to the pattern, she could make different choices in her life.

If, like Samantha, your life problems center on interpersonal relationships, there are some things you need to know. First, give yourself credit for meeting your basic needs of food, water, shelter, and safety (see *Own your problems in living*, page 34). Second, you are trying to meet your social need for connection to others through your pursuit of relationships, and they are necessary for meaningful living. Don't beat yourself up for needing relationships. Instead, evaluate the effectiveness of your behaviors in those relationships. Are they giving you the kind of connection you need? If not, it's time for new strategies. Third, relationships are immensely complicated because there are two people involved, and you can only control yourself.

Use the change, discernment, and acceptance skills (see *Understand the control problem*, page 18) to increase your social effectiveness. At best, we can only influence other people's behavior. Are you trying to manage people (your children, your partner, your boss, your co-workers, or your clients) who are out of your control? This is where effective discernment is required. You cannot force someone to love you or value the things you do.

At best, we can only influence other people's behavior. Are you trying to manage people (your children, your partner, your boss, your co-workers, or your clients) who are out of your control?

For example, if it is a priority for you to live in an orderly home, but you live with a partner who does not place the same value on organization, you have a dilemma. Objectively, this is an area of poor fit. This does not mean that one of you is right and the other wrong (see *Stop being* right, *and start understanding,* page 42). The two of you are just different.

Let's say that one day, you notice small piles of your partner's dirty clothes scattered on the floor in random places around the house you share. Anger swells inside of you. As a skilled manager of your mind, you reflect and decode the message of

Connection to others

Impulsively reacting

your anger (see *Know the products of your mind*, page 27). Your anger reminds you of your preference for an uncluttered floor. In this situation, use the discernment skill to determine what is within your control and what is not. You can control your behavior and influence your thoughts and feelings. You could choose to pick up the clothes yourself or accept this difference as part of having this relationship and all that you get from it. You can attempt to influence the situation by telling your partner how important it is to you, asking for a change in his or her behavior, and offering to do something your partner values if he or she picks up the dirty clothes. You could choose to end the relationship, or you might decide to suffer in the situation without doing anything. You cannot, however, force your partner to change. People will only change if they choose it and then work through the process themselves (see *Change is a process, not an event*, page 44).

Healthy relationships, as infinitely rewarding as they are, always require work. Recent research studies from marital expert John Gottman, PhD, have shown that healthy relationships may even promote physical wellness in partners.

What are the recurring patterns in your relationships? If you ever wonder, "Why is this always happening to me?" determine your contributions to the relationship problems you have. Are some of your behaviors causing friction with your partner? Use the reflect skill to determine the function of that behavior. It could be an attempt to meet your needs or to solve a problem. Could you do that with new choices that are effective and do not damage your relationship? Remember, the goal is to effectively meet your social needs (see *Own your problems in living*, page 34), and this is impossible when you are living the control problem in your relationships.

When the control problem is in your relationship, you can:

Change the relationship

Accept the situation using the acceptance skill

Influence how you feel about the situation

Do nothing and continue to suffer

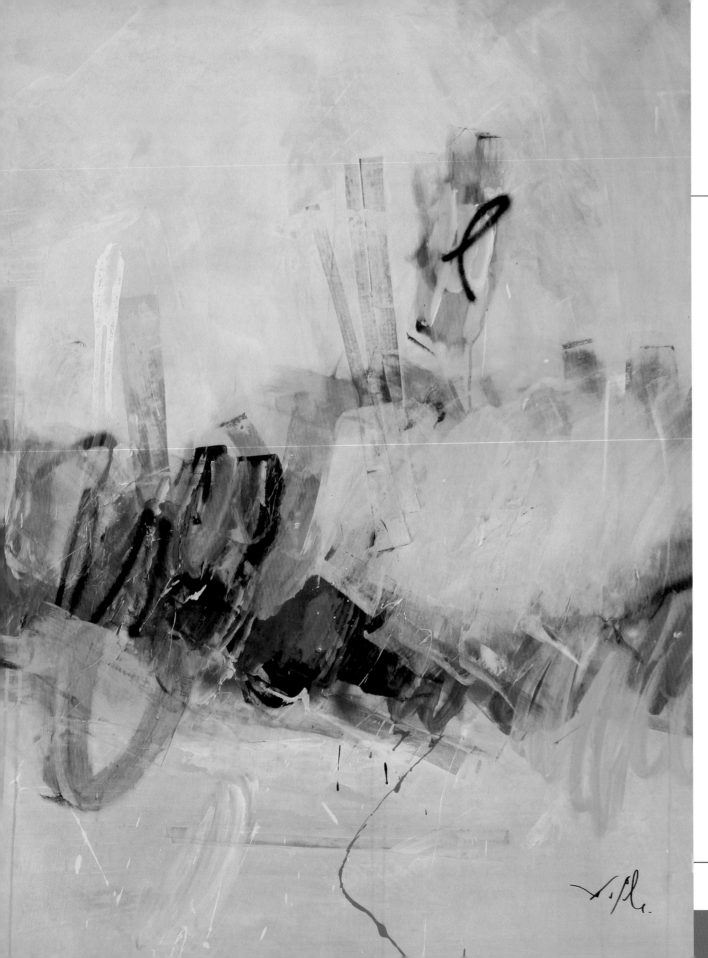

Many of the truths we cling to depend greatly on our own point of view.
—Obi Wan Kenobi, *Star Wars: A New Hope*, George Lucas

We see the world and the people in it through lenses tempered by our own individual life experiences, so it is impossible for two people to see everything exactly the same way. I often illustrate this to my clients by explaining how each of us has a different experience during the same therapy session. Problems in living arise in our interpersonal relationships when we judge other people's experiences as wrong. This mistake is compounded when we try to assert our point of view as right for them. This type of judgmental behavior will sabotage your efforts to meet your social needs (see *Own your problems in living*, page 34).

Not all judgments are problematic. In fact, we make judgments to survive the day. Imagine being a pedestrian trying to cross a busy street. I usually make the judgment to walk when I see the white shape in the crosswalk sign and stop when

No two people see anything exactly the same way

Stop being *RIGHT*, and start understanding

I see the red one. You have probably made similar decisions in the past. These are automatic judgments made from a state of unconscious competence (see *Learn the learning curve*, page 48). Keep making these effective judgments; ignore any judgments that come to your mind that are based on distorted assessments of yourself or others. Accepting ineffective, judgmental thoughts leads to biased opinions and stereotypes. Actions taken based on these disparaging beliefs are often folly. The story of my client, Tom, shows how ineffective judgments can derail relationships.

> *Accepting ineffective, judgmental thoughts leads to biased opinions and stereotypes. Actions taken based on these disparaging beliefs are often folly.*

Tom is a driven, well-educated man with strong beliefs about what is "right" and what is "wrong." He sizes up situations quickly and takes decisive actions. This strength served Tom quite well in his education and career. In fact, this capacity was a pillar of Tom's self-image as a strong, independent man. So it was quite a blow for Tom to learn that his strength of making quick, decisive judgments was a big part of the problems with his son. He was at his wit's end and sought my help because his sixteen-year-old son, Alex, was emotionally overwhelmed and overwhelming. They yelled at each other every week, and Tom feared that their arguments could become physical.

Tom parented with the same strategies that served him well in everything else: quick judgments followed by definitive decisions. He judged his son's choices through the lens of his own sense of right and wrong. Tom described his son's friends as not good enough, snobby, and racist. They never came from the right kind of families. His son's decisions were "naive" and his comments "ridiculous." Even the television programs he watched were "nauseating," and his lack of interest in current events made Tom worry that his son was "shallow." When I pointed out the pattern of negative judgments to Tom, he heard it as an attack. He told me how good his judgment was, how he wanted to protect his son, and that he was only looking out for him. All of this was true from Tom's point of view, but his strategy was not working. In fact, it had damaged his relationship with his son.

We all have judgmental thoughts. The trick is not to immediately believe or buy them. Tom learned to utilize the mind management skills of mind monitoring, pause, and reflection to have his initial judgments but react to his son in a curious manner. For example, the next time Alex watched a reality television show, Tom initially thought, "This show is evidence of the decline of Western civilization," but he said to his son, "What do you like most about this show?" Tom listened to his son with the purpose of understanding how his son views the world. This kind of interaction, over time, rebuilt the relationship between father and son.

When you find yourself locked into a repeating negative cycle with someone else, be openly curious about his or her point of view. Engage people in discussions with open-ended questions like: *How did you come to that decision? What do you like about that? Will you share your thoughts on that? How do you feel about it?* Understanding someone does not mean that you are obligated to agree with them. Improved understanding, however, will lead to more effective relationships.

Which of your judgmental thoughts interferes with your quality of life?

CHANGE IS A PROCESS, NOT AN EVENT

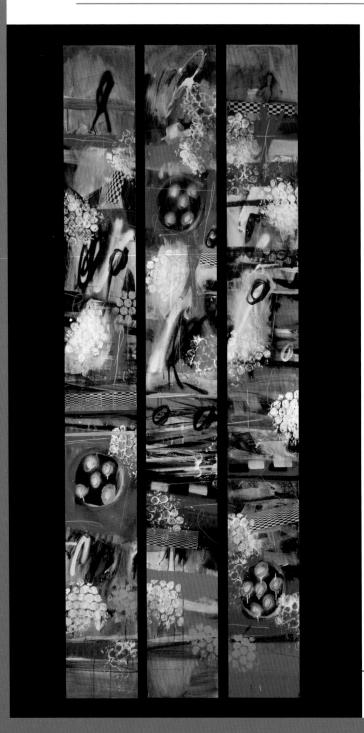

Change process triptych

Why does a father of two in his mid-forties light up a cigarette on the way home from meeting with the doctor who just diagnosed his early-stage emphysema? Why would a man with chronic arthritis and back pain keep eating fast food that makes that excess thirty pounds a permanent fixture on his body, despite the doctor's advice to lose weight? People who "know better" continue harmful behaviors because information alone does not convince them to choose change. Substantial life changes require people to go through an entire psychological process. It's not like turning on a light switch.

> *Substantial life changes require people to go through an entire psychological process. It's not like turning on a light switch.*

Change as a process is quite different than some of the messages we receive from mass media. Reality TV programs appear to show people completely altering their bodies within twelve episodes, unruly pets being tamed with a few whispers, and lives changing with a DNA test result and some harsh words exchanged during a fifteen-minute segment between commercial breaks. A corporate giant once told us to "just do it," and while "doing" is crucial, it is only a part of the entire process. Skipping some of the stages of change only prolongs the time until success occurs.

Parents, this is why your kids don't automatically change when you give them advice. Absent a condition like bipolar mania, human beings do not wake up one day and arbitrarily change the color of the living room, cut down how much alcohol they drink, or start a new relationship. Change is a process, not an event. The duration of the process varies from person to person and situation to situation.

Change comes in seven distinct stages, as defined by researchers James O. Prochaska, PhD, and Carlo C. DiClemente, PhD. These stages are pre-contemplation, contemplation, preparation, action, maintenance, relapse, and termination.

Pre-contemplation is when you have no awareness of a need for a change. Some triggering event will shift you from pre-contemplation to contemplation. **Contemplation** is when you're thinking about making a change. The diagnosis of emphysema did not motivate the fictional father mentioned above to stop smoking, because that would be the action phase, but it did move him into contemplation. The **preparation** phase of change is when you get all the information and resources you need to make a change in your life. For our smoker, this could look like buying smoke cessation aids like patches, gums, or medications, or finding local smoking cessation support groups and getting their schedules. When you were trying to make a life change, did anyone ever tell you something like "just get over it" or "think about those less fortunate than you"? This well-meaning advice is only effective at this exact point in your personal change process. If you are almost done getting ready, the right advice can initiate the next phase in the change. If you are not ready, however, no advice will jump you into action. **Action** is when your change in behavior is happening and can be noticed by other people. People move to the action stage of

Information alone does not convince them to choose change

change when living life with the status quo becomes too uncomfortable or painful to tolerate any longer. The **maintenance** phase of change is when your actions have been successful and the new behavior is holding steady. At this point, our smoker is not smoking anymore. In chemical dependency treatment, relapse is part of recovery, and the axiom applies to change processes, too. In the **relapse** phase of change, the smoker starts sneaking occasional cigarettes again. Do not beat yourself up when your old behaviors come sneaking back into your life. It's part of successful change. Notice the relapse, and then bring your attention back to the action and maintenance phases. Once you have gone through each of the first six phases as many times as you need to, for as long as it takes, the change process ends with **termination**.

If you flip back to the table of contents for a moment, you'll find that the sections of *The Art of Meaningful Living* are organized according to the change process. We made this decision when organizing the book because there is no greater change than choosing your passions over your fears. **Start** represents the contemplation phase when you're thinking about committing to this process. **Wisdom** is the preparation you need before action can happen. **Action** contains some behaviors that can help you live your meaningful life each day. The

Facilitating changes

information in **Resilience** helps you when avoidant living reappears in your choices. Finally, **The Art of Meaningful Lives** profiles people who are living their passions.

Let's consider what we know about you. You have moved beyond the contemplation phase of a change process and have been considering making changes in your life. We know this because you are reading this book. This change is a marathon, not a sprint. Enjoy some of the present moments along the way.

These kinds of choices

The seven phases of the change process:

Pre-contemplation: "Problem? What problem?"

Contemplation: "Oh, that problem. I should really do something about that."

Preparation: "I'm getting ready to do something about that."

Action: "Now I am doing something about that."

Maintenance: "Hey, look at me! I'm still doing it."

Relapse: "Oh, no, I am off track."

Termination: "I did it!"

You experience the learning curve each time you try something new. It's a process, like change (see *Change is a process, not an event*, page 44), of varied duration. The four stages of the learning curve are unconscious incompetence, conscious incompetence, conscious competence, and unconscious competence.

You experience the learning curve each time you try something new. It's a process, like change, of varied duration.

Unconscious incompetence is like blissful ignorance. You do not know what you do not know so there is no discomfort until you experience a wake-up call. A poor performance review, a blaring car horn, a failing grade, or an angry partner are all things that can teach you what you do not know. These are pushes into **conscious incompetence**. It is this second learning phase that hurts. Acknowledging your ignorance is humbling and can be embarrassing and frustrating. If you have an avoidant style, the pain of conscious incompetence keeps you from trying new

Unconscious incompetence is blissful ignorance

things (see *Choose your style of living*, page 10). You toil in conscious incompetence as long as it takes. Endure the discomfort and eventually you become skilled enough to be a **conscious competent**. The third stage of the learning curve requires focused attention until the new behavior becomes habitual. This is when you know what you know, but it is not yet automatic. Once your new skills are second nature, you have completed the learning curve by moving into **unconscious competence**.

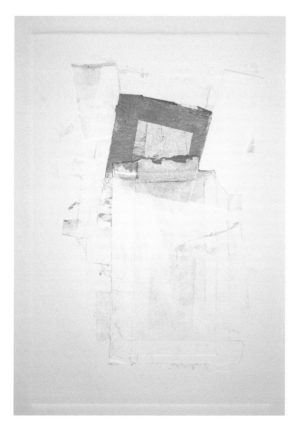

Remember learning to ride a bicycle

Remember learning to ride a bicycle? At first, you didn't know about bikes. Then you got a wake-up call. Maybe you saw the big kids in the neighborhood riding their two-wheelers. Whatever it was, something convinced you to learn how to ride a bike. Maybe you started with training wheels as you struggled with conscious incompetence. Eventually, those wheels came off, but you probably needed to fall down a few times. Those painful scraped knees were a necessary part of the learning process. Eventually, you found your balance. At first, it was wobbly, but then you held the bike steady. This took concentration and marked your progression to conscious competence. You had to concentrate to stay upright for a while, but in due course, you were riding with no hands. This was the end of that learning curve. Think of any new circumstance as learning to ride a bike all over again.

Choosing a meaningful lifestyle is courageous because it requires embracing each stage of the learning curve repeatedly. As with change, you cannot skip any phase of the learning curve. It is tempting to give up during the pain of conscious incompetence or conscious competence, but don't. Instead, assign a new meaning to that discomfort. It is a sign of learning and growth. The awkwardness and pain of the learning curve are signs that you're moving closer to your meaningful life.

The four phases of the learning curve:

Unconscious incompetence: "I don't know what I don't know."

Conscious incompetence: "I know what I don't know, and that hurts."

Conscious competence: "I know what I know if I concentrate on it."

Unconscious competence: "I know what I know without giving it a second thought."

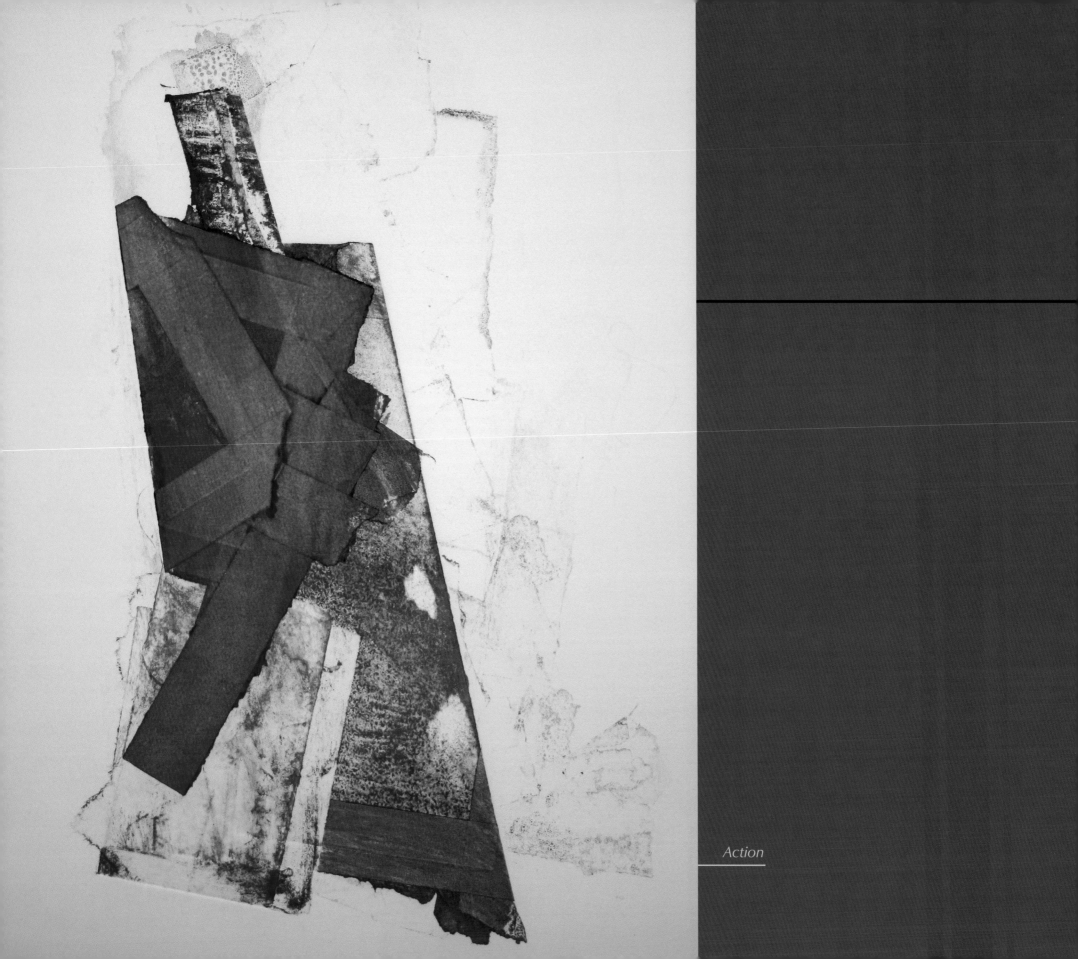

Action

ACTION

Action is essential to building your meaningful life. While developing wisdom is an internal process, action is behavior that other people can see or notice. After you have gotten ready to change, it is time to move.

DEFINE YOUR PASSIONS

Your passions are people, activities, and things that fully engage the rational and emotional sides of your mind. When you are passionate about something, you know it and you feel it. Notice how your perception of time changes when you are fully engaged with your passion. Athletes refer to this as being "in the zone." Time can speed up or slow down. This experience is a clue that you are in your passion. In meaningful living, your personal passions become the basis for your daily life choices.

In meaningful living, your personal passions become the basis for your daily life choices.

Since you are the expert on what you think and how you feel, you're the only person who can correctly define your passions. In adulthood, you get to define your priorities and how you spend your time. That's right: you get to pick. Your passions cannot be better or worse than anyone else's. They're just different. This is liberating, especially if you were programmed with strict definitions of what is the right or wrong way to do things. While you may choose to keep some values espoused by your family of origin, you may choose to let go of others. It's your life. Choose what's a good fit for you and leave what's not. Stop responding to the judgmental thoughts that come with comparing yourself to others, and reflect on your interest in what you're doing. Are you truly passionate about your career, your relationships, and your life?

One way to define your passions is to prioritize the following ten elements of meaningful living. The elements are inspired by the ideas of psychologist Kelly G. Wilson, PhD. Again, one element is not intrinsically better than another; they're just different. Take as much time as you need with the following pages. Use your

Happening around you

entire managed mind as you read the text describing each element and consider the accompanying images. From your wise mind (see *Reflect on your mind*, page 24), identify your personal prioritized elements of meaningful living. You don't have to embrace all ten areas. In fact, the purpose within the context of meaningful living is to focus on the one, two, or three elements that inspire you most, and then act accordingly. You might feel grief that you can't do it all. This is an unpleasant reality, but accepting this disappointment is choosing meaningful living over avoidant living (see *Choose your style of living*, page 10).

Notice your breathing

Befriend:

Friends are the family of your choosing. Friendships are far more than casual acquaintances; they require care and attention. When your friends and social life are central to your meaningful life, the effort feeds both you and your friend, plus the relationship between the two of you.

Grow:

Expand your range of experience to develop yourself. Growth is characterized by continuing education, training in new specialties, experiencing other cultures, and learning new skills. Yes, growth can be painful, but when continual development is central to your meaningful life, the experience is worth it.

Heal:

Care for yourself physically and emotionally because life can be difficult. You will need to heal from its experiences and lessons. Heal with adequate sleep, a nourishing diet, physical activity, healthy relationships, and professional treatments. This passion establishes your self-care as an equal priority with the needs of others.

Nurture:

When the growth and development of others provides you with fulfillment, nurturing is your passion. Parenting certainly can provide you a chance to nurture, but having children is only one of many ways to fulfill this passion. Nurture through mentoring or coaching. Care for other living things, like pets or plants. When nurturing is your passion, you nourish others to nourish yourself.

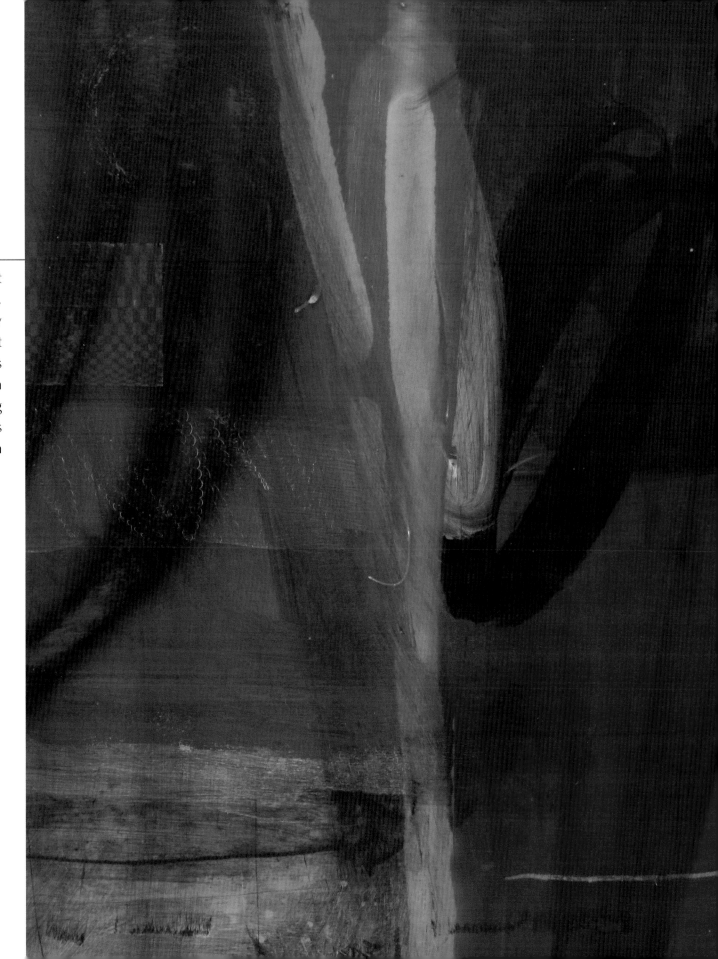

Partner:

To partner is to join another person in an intimate relationship. These relationships are embodied by public commitments that unite one human being to another. Intimate partnerships require you to love, desire, and long for another person. Successful partnerships also require consistent care with each person able to be both *I* and *we* within the relationship.

Play:

Play is activity with the purpose of relaxing, amusing, and delighting you. If you have forgotten how to play, spend time watching young children; they're the experts. Forms of play are only limited by your imagination. Adults play in their intimate relationships, hobbies, and pastimes. Whether you enjoy going to the movies, traveling to new places, or collecting vintage toys, it is all recreation, or a form of play.

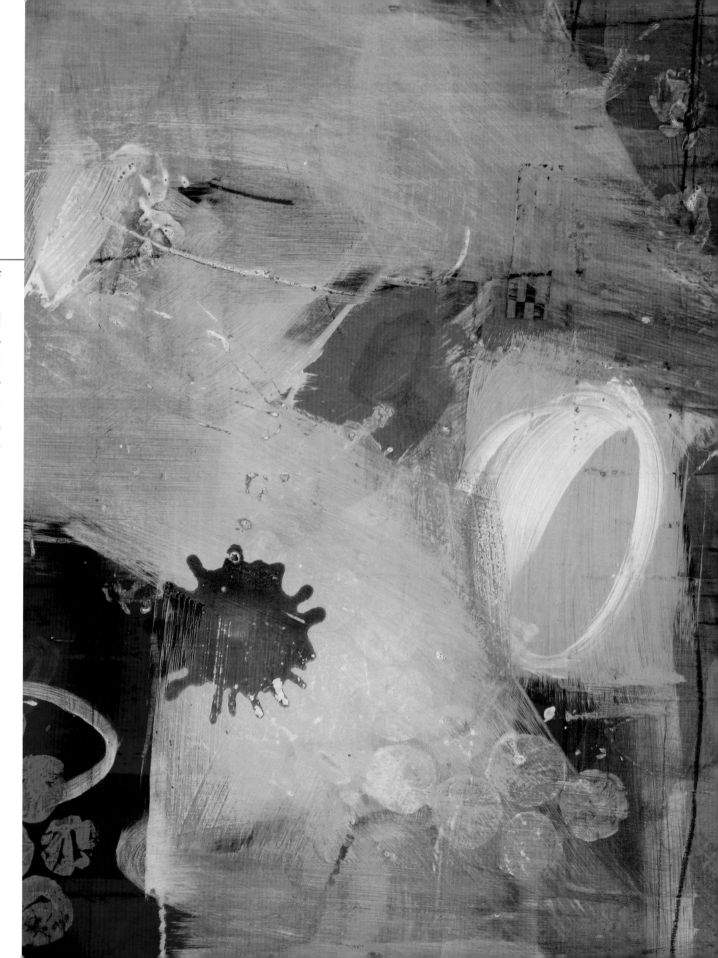

Relate:

This element of meaningful living connects you with who you came from: your family of origin. When connecting with the family you were adopted or born into is a passion, invest energy and time into your relationships with Mom, Dad, Brother, Sister, Cousin, or other kin who are important to you.

Serve:

Serving a community, large or small, can bring great satisfaction and meaning. When actions of service consistently give you energy and contentment, serving is one of your passions. Serving in the military or government service, joining in professional organizations or activist coalitions, and volunteering in nonprofit organizations, neighborhood associations, or school committees are different ways to pursue a passion of service.

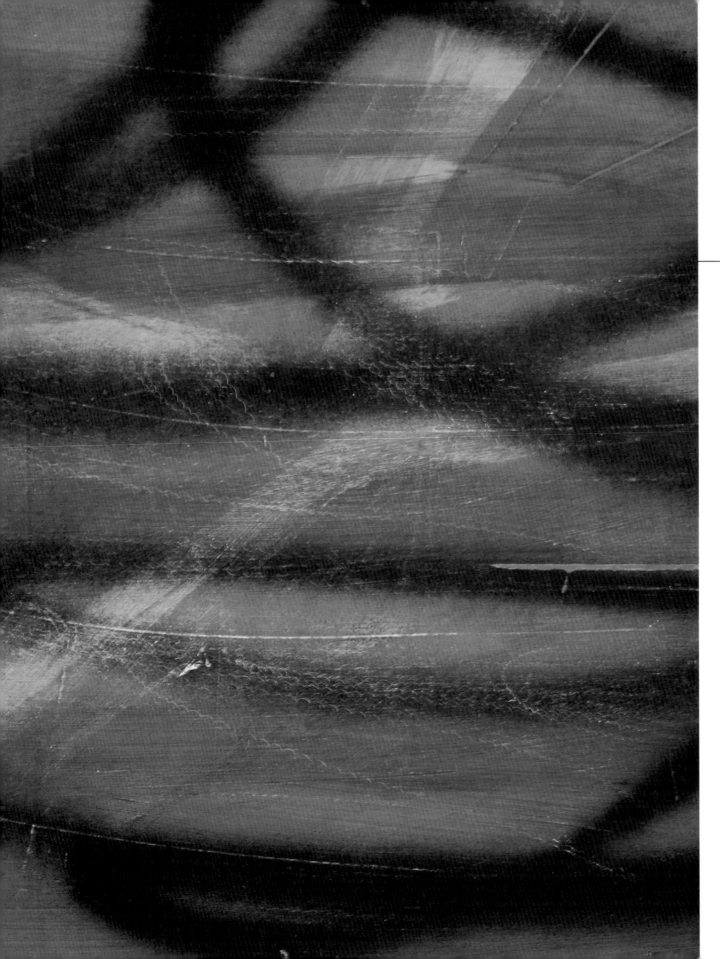

Transcend:

Transcendence is the ability to exist above and apart from the material world. Spirituality is transcendent. Your spirituality may include organized religion, or it may not. Regardless, you transcend when you believe in a power greater than yourself that connects all of us. Pursue this universal force by being involved with a church, a twelve-step program, or an organized meditation with a focus on connecting with a larger world. Creativity is also transcendent. Be open to your creative energy by transcending, or rising above, your day-to-day struggles.

Work:

When work is your passion, it's more than earning a living; it becomes a calling. Careers and professional personas are often people's defining characteristics. Providing for yourself and others is a way to build self-esteem and confidence in your capabilities. Financial security can also be the means by which other areas of meaningful living can have expression.

Ultimately, meaningful living requires looking into your heart and finding your passions among these ten choices. What is your mind telling you about the elements of meaningful living? What are your thoughts, feelings, memories, urges, and sensations? Each reaction gives you information about what is valuable to you and what is not. A thought such as "Why did they put this on the list?" lets you know this element might be a lower priority for you. A memory of the joy you experienced in school when you finally grasped a complex concept might clue you into "growth" as a meaningful life pursuit. Do any images flash into your mind as you think of friends, family members, or intimate partners? If so, what are the accompanying feelings or sensations? Listen to the products of your mind and then interpret them (see *Know the products of your mind*, page 27).

Now that you have defined your passions, it's time to live them. Your life's journey is a road paved with the choices you make each day. If most of your daily choices are impulsive and reactionary, then you will never reach your meaningful life. Instead, hold your passionate elements in your mind as you make decisions both big and small. Choose what best fits your passions, and your road will lead toward meaning instead of away from it.

Perhaps you are remembering past experiences

Can change relationships

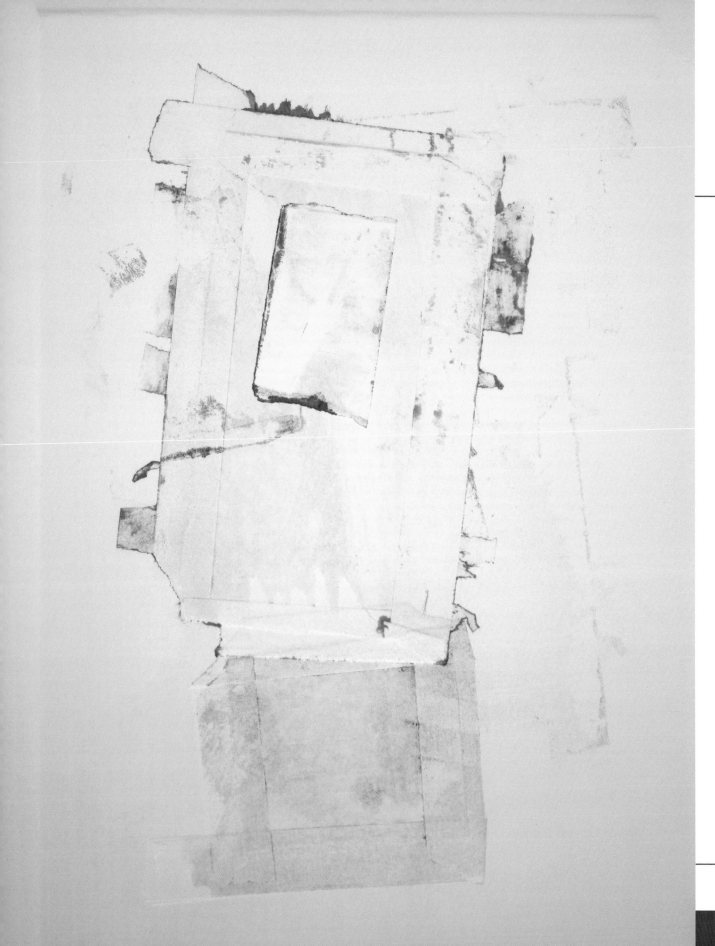

Pursue your passions today. As long as you draw breath, it is not too late to do something meaningful. Your journey toward meaningful living continues as you make daily decisions that represent your elements of meaningful living in ways both large and small.

Consider how you have spent your time during the past seven days. Remember your two or three most important elements of meaningful living (see *Define your passions*, page 52). Did you spend the majority of your time directly involved in your passions? If not, what took up most of your time? Sadly, you might be spending most of your time working when what you truly value is nurturing. You might value friends, yet your time is consumed with family obligations. Significant discrepancy between what is meaningful to you and how you spend your time is a warning sign of quiet desperation (see *Choose your style of living*, page 10).

Meaningful living requires that your time be spent congruently with your passions

Spend your time on your passions

Significant discrepancy between what is meaningful to you and how you spend your time is a warning sign of quiet desperation.

What you value most may not fit your current life circumstances. For example, partnering may be most important to you, yet you are single. Nurturing might be the most important thing in your world, yet you do not have children. Your life in the present moment is what it is. Accept that. You can only be where you are right now, armed with important information about what to move toward in your life. Do not judge yourself harshly if your time allocation is disproportionate to your passionate elements. Just notice that fact as you move into the conscious incompetence phase of the change process and get ready to change.

You may choose to invest your time in one area for a while in order to move into living your life the way you choose. This is a way to improve your overall quality of

Live your passions

life going forward. One of my clients had a majority of his previous week dedicated to healing, which was a low priority on his list. His most valued life activities involved family and spirituality, but he had spent

little time on them. Rather than beating himself up, which was his unmanaged mind's pattern, we simply ascribed informational value to the incongruence. To learn from this information, he had to understand the context of his behavior in order to work on his self-care, which was why he specifically came to me in the first place.

At the end of every twenty-four-hour period, your existence stands for something, whether or not you are aware of it. Focus your wise mind on the following question as you end every day: What did my life stand for today?

Search for an answer that could fit into a phrase or two. Take no more than three minutes for this exercise because you will overthink the question otherwise. Reflect on your answer to determine if your day stood for your elements of meaningful living.

Being nonjudgmental is especially important in this exercise. Just be aware of the information, and respond with considered choices. Be curious. What did you learn? What got in your way? What can you change to make tomorrow more meaningful?

BE NOW

Our minds may ruminate about the past and worry about the future, but we can only live in the present moment. In every instant, events are occurring on multiple levels. Let's build your awareness around and within you. Right now, you are reading words and looking at images. These are clearly outside of you. As you become aware of these concepts, there are dozens of responses happening within your mind and body. You may be thinking, "This is the most interesting book I have ever read." You may feel curious or excited. You might even want to buy another copy of this book! Perhaps you are remembering past experiences like a lecture you heard in a psychology class years ago. Meanwhile, your body is full of physical sensations.

You might be hungry or thirsty, hot or cold. All of these could be happening in this one moment. Bring your focus to what is happening in your mind and body right now. Remember, there is no wrong way to do this.

Take sixty seconds, and notice all of the activity within your mind and body.

There are also dozens of things happening around you at any moment. Some you might notice and others might pass unconsciously. Still, some part of your mind registers these events even if we never realize it.

Take sixty seconds, and notice what is happening around you.

What did you notice? Observe what caught your attention, once you brought your focus to it. Did you notice anything that might have slipped your awareness earlier?

Mastering the ability to be mindful of what is going on around and within you will help you make more informed choices.

Mindfulness exercises such as these are being used increasingly in evidence-based psychotherapies such as Acceptance and Commitment Therapy (ACT) and Dialectical Behavior Therapy (DBT). Jon Kabat-Zinn, PhD, has defined mindfulness as "paying attention in a particular way, on purpose, in the present moment, and non-judgmentally." Clinical studies by Kabat-Zinn and his colleagues have shown that consistently applied mindfulness exercises have clinically significant effects on brain activity in areas typically associated with positive emotional states and increase

New practices

the effectiveness of the immune system. Mastering the ability to be mindful of what is going on around and within you will help you make more informed choices. It will also allow you to endure discomfort when necessary and enjoy aspects of present moment living that you would have missed earlier.

Observation skills

Live in the present moment

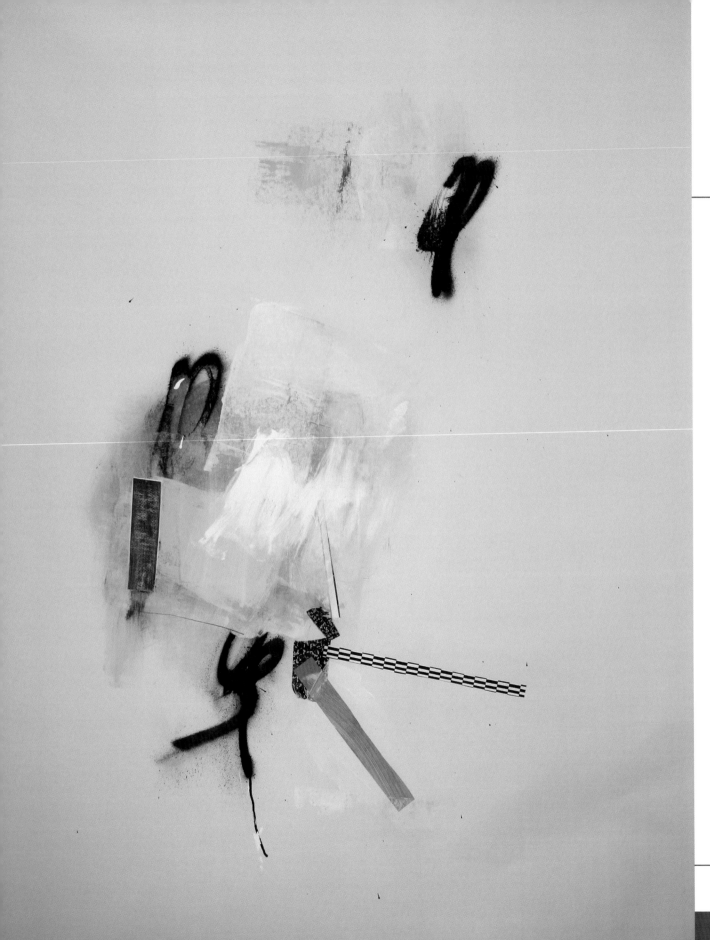

We are, at least, the sum of our experiences. Unfortunately, life is not like a buffet line where we can choose what we want to have and leave what we don't like. We get it all: the good, the bad, the ugly, and the boring. What we do with it is most important. Meaningful living comes from moving in the direction of what is uniquely valuable to you while also dealing directly with what life throws your way.

Sometimes, this means we have to deal with pain. Recent studies have shown that patients report a decrease in the intensity of physical pain caused by non-life-threatening injuries if they focus on the sensation for a limited period of time rather than ignoring it. One doctor explained that if you bring your focus to the wound or injury, your mind is satisfied that it has done its job of bringing the problem to your awareness, which allows the pain to recede. Avoidance can be adaptive, but once an injury has occurred, ignoring the pain prolongs suffering.

Emotions are not bad, emotions do not make you weak

HAVE ALL OF YOUR EXPERIENCES

Having your experiences without buying into the judgmental thoughts about them increases your ability to tolerate distress and shortens the time you will suffer.

When it comes to our emotional lives, we tend to avoid circumstances that we label as negative. It is the labeling that we can control. Labeling is another version of judging. Eliminate the judgment, and focus on the emotional pain. Feel it. Describe it. Embrace it. Only then will it recede. To avoid thinking of the emotional pain once it has happened will only prolong the suffering. Having your experiences without buying into the judgmental thoughts about them increases your ability to tolerate distress and shortens the time you will suffer. Steven Hayes, PhD, often uses the following exercise to illustrate that point.

Using a watch, time how long you can hold your breath.

How long could you go without exhaling?

Repeat the exercise and focus on noticing all the different things that occur in your mind as you hold your breath. Your mind may give you thoughts such as "I can't hold my breath very long," plus feelings like nervousness and anxiety along with various unrelated memories, sensations, and urges. Simply notice them and move on to the next experience.

Using a watch, time how long you can hold your breath while observing the products of your mind.

How long did you hold your breath the second time? Usually, people hold their breath longer when using these observation skills. We can tolerate painful experiences more easily by focusing on them rather than avoiding them. Learn to observe your experience of emotional pain during periods of inevitable suffering in your life while continuing to make life choices

according to your elements of meaningful living (see *Define your passions*, page 52).

When you are open to your experiences, you can react in many ways, given the circumstance and the outcome that you want. Embrace all of your experiences, and

Circumstances we label as negative

Patterns might start like this

respond with actions that are consistent with your personal values. If you are sad, be sad. Observe where you feel your sadness within your body. Assign a color, shape, and size to your experience of sadness. If you are crying, observe the physical sensation of the tears upon your cheeks. Report what is happening to your breathing. Is it shallow or deep, rapid or slow?

Practice truly having all of your emotional experiences until they pass. Experts in exposure and response prevention therapy say that it takes an average of ninety minutes to have an intense emotional experience, feel the feeling, then calm down without any outside help. Others say that a single emotional experience lasts about fifteen seconds without another cue from either our minds or the environment (this is why the boundary setting is so important). Your own experiences will probably last longer than fifteen seconds but less than ninety minutes. The important thing is that if you focus on the emotional experience, the intensity will come down on its own as long as you don't experience triggers repeatedly.

Burying your emotional reactions never works. Buried feelings will come out somehow, even sideways. They do not stay buried. You might find yourself yelling at your kids when you are really angry with your boss, or you might get depressed when you are really angry with your family. If you were taught that emotions were wrong or bad, this can be an old program to challenge. Those feelings are saying something to you, and you need to uncover what that is. After you have awareness, it is important to put the feelings back where they belong. If you are angry with your boss or your family, perhaps it's time to set boundaries and exercise self-care. This will create energy for your meaningful living. Embrace your experiences of the internal and external worlds. Listen for what they are telling you, and choose responses that fit your meaningful life.

Triggering more flooding

MAKE EFFECTIVE DECISIONS

Live your passions through the decisions you make each day. Once you build your awareness, the sheer number of daily decisions you make may be surprising. While some decisions do not require great contemplation, others are more complex. When you face a decision with any degree of difficulty, your personal passions can guide you to the path toward your meaningful life (see *Define your passions*, page 52).

Once, I asked a client, Ray, to consider why he drank alcohol to the point of intoxication, despite recent legal troubles. His first response was a judgment: "Because I'm stupid." Ray and I explored that possibility and looked at the evidence for and against. He is a college graduate with experience working in a variety of businesses since he was an adolescent. Given this data, I asked him if he really believed he was stupid. He said no. I agreed, so we ruled out stupidity as an option. Then we continued to speculate on why an intelligent man might engage in this drinking behavior and came up with a new possibility. His emotional mind was dominating him. Fueled by alcohol, Ray's loud emotional mind convinced him that his friends would forget about him if he did not party with them. He was solving the imagined problem of abandonment

Small and progressive adjustments

by going to bars when his friends did and drinking alcohol when they did. His solution was effective, in that his friends could not forget about him, but it also had the high costs of legal trouble and problems at work. Ironically, when Ray was intoxicated, he often behaved in offensive ways that alienated the friends that he was trying to keep.

After reflecting on the situation, Ray chose a new strategy to solve his problem. He enlisted his friends in the problem-solving process by talking openly with them about his desire to remain part of the group while cutting back on his drinking. Ray and his friends now go for an extended lunch at least once a week, and they avoid nightclubs. Ray has chosen an effective strategy to maintain his friendships, which is congruent with his most important element of meaningful living: befriend.

Adequately nourished

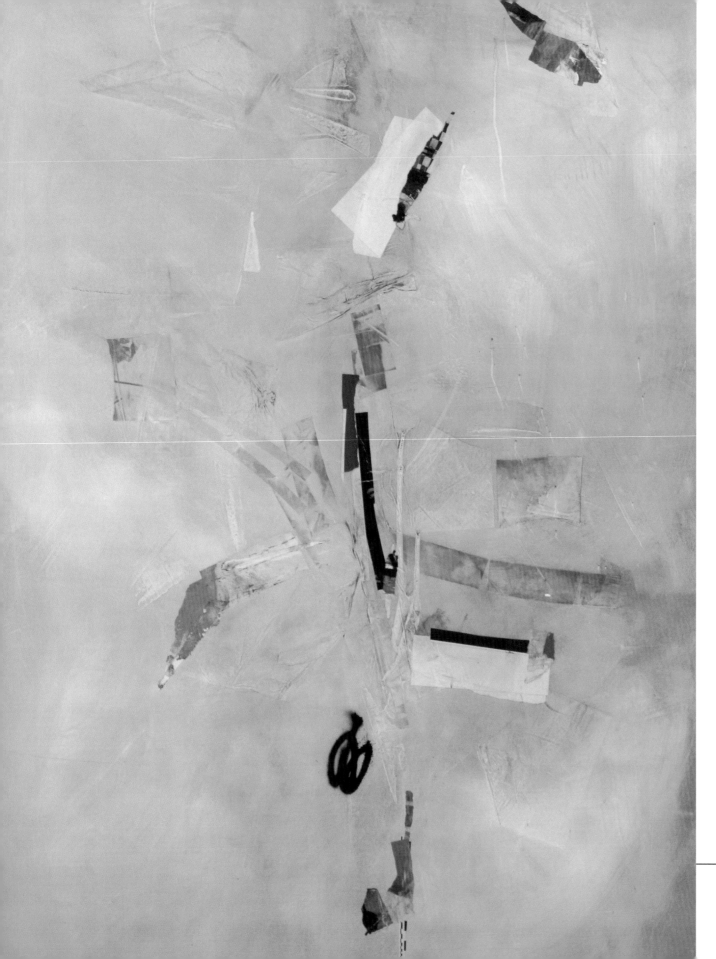

Your prioritized elements of meaningful living are the compass that will guide your decisions toward your meaningful life.

When you are facing a difficult decision, use your pause and reflect skills to slow down (see *Mind management*, page 22). This will prevent you from acting too quickly from only the emotional side of your mind. After any emotional flooding has passed, define the problem. You will rarely make effective decisions if you do not know the problem you are trying to solve. After you have defined the problem, develop possible solutions. Do not rule any strategy out immediately. The goal is to give you options. This type of brainstorming is often effective in collaboration with a nonjudgmental friend or family member. With the potential strategies in mind, recall

Recall your personal passions

your personal passions. Your prioritized elements of meaningful living are the compass that will guide your decisions toward your meaningful life. A client, Erica, recently used her elements of meaningful living to help her decide to set limits at work. This gave her more time and energy to connect with family members. Basing decisions on the elements of your meaningful life is how you can put your wisdom into action each day.

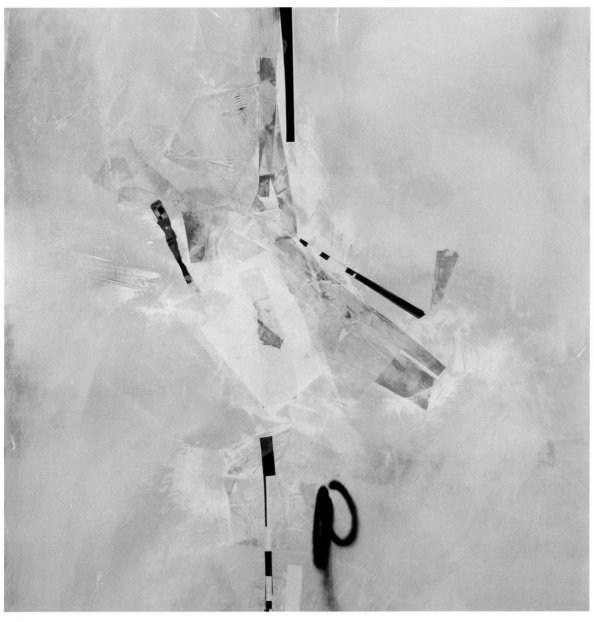

Effective decisions

Steps for effective decision making:

Stop any emotional flooding.

Define the problem precisely.

Evaluate the effectiveness of your current problem-solving strategies.

Determine any negative results from your current strategy.

Decide if you want to change problem-solving strategies.

Brainstorm alternative solutions, if necessary.

Get input from capable, trusted others for more possible solutions.

Recall your prioritized elements of meaningful living.

Choose the strategy that best fits your elements of meaningful living.

After time, evaluate your results and reconsider if necessary.

Indifference is the opposite of passion. Acts of indifference are the actions that drain your time and energy without adding to your meaningful life. If most of your time is filled with acts of indifference instead of passion, you will despair. Once you know what you are passionate about, focus on eliminating that which you are indifferent about. In the age of multitasking, downsizing, cross-functioning, and dual-income families, we are busier than ever before. Reflect on this question: Is your daily life full of acts of passion or indifference?

If most of your time is filled with acts of indifference instead of passion, you will despair. Once you know what you are passionate about, focus on eliminating that which you are indifferent about.

What got in your way

REDUCE AND REFRAME ACTS OF INDIFFERENCE

Acts of indifference

Reducing the number of acts of indifference in your daily life frees time and energy for your passions.

Eliminating some acts of indifference can be difficult to do for several reasons. We are naturally drawn to what is familiar by our human need for self-esteem. Feeling capable builds healthy esteem, so it makes sense that we would keep doing what we already know how to do. When you do what you know how to do and not what you are passionate about, your growth will hit an artificial ceiling. Further, if what you know how to do does not add meaning to your life, you are set up for quiet desperation. Often we

are drawn into acts of indifference because of other people's priorities. Remember that our minds are programmed early on in our lives (see *Your most personal computer*, page 22). Consider if you are doing things in life because they are important to you or because they are important to someone else. You cannot have your full meaningful life when you are living other people's elements instead of your own.

One client, Brandon, had been an accountant since he graduated from college five years before we started working together. He went into accounting because his father was a businessman, and it seemed to Brandon that was the kind of job a man was "supposed to have." He had been promoted regularly and was being offered another step up the corporate ladder. If he took it, it would mean a move across the country away from his family of origin. We defined his prioritized elements of meaningful living, and his original family was significantly more important to him than his work. When we examined his own interests, we discovered that one of the reasons that he did not value work highly was because he hated his job. In Brandon's mind, work was defined by his father's career, and he actually hated accounting. We expanded his view of work and defined it by his own interests. Brandon

was actually very interested in the creative fields of interior design and graphic design. He decided to decline the promotion, stay close to his family of origin, and lean on them for support as he made a career change into a creative field during the next two years. Like Brandon, you can develop a plan to reduce or eliminate the indifferences from your life.

Another way to eliminate acts of indifference from your life is to reframe them in terms of your elements of meaningful living. Reframing is changing how you think of a given situation. For example, if your personal passions are play, partnering, and nurturing, and you are the breadwinner for a family of four with a mortgage, two car payments, and school tuition bills, quitting your job is not a viable option. You can, however, change the meaning assigned to your work. Your work can also be viewed as a means of nurturing your children and supporting your partner.

What life activities can you reframe in terms of your passions?

We explored the patterns

Establish accountability for yourself

There must be consequences for our choices if we are to learn from them, so accountability is a vital component of meaningful living. Experiencing the consequences of our choices helps us gain motivation. Some consequences are natural.

Establish accountability

Psychologist Rion Hart, PhD, says people will change when staying the same becomes too painful to accept any longer. In this context, physical and psychological pain can be reframed as catalysts for change. Other consequences are provided by the public commitments we make. Marriage vows, made between intimate partners in front of witnesses, are public acceptances of responsibilities to each other and the partnership. They establish accountability. Participants in Alcoholics Anonymous are accountable to the group, their sponsors, and themselves. My coaching clients work with me in part because their change efforts are more effective when we consistently set goals, review their progress, and acknowledge what they have learned before making new commitments.

Make commitments by setting specific outcome goals for yourself. Your goal can be external, such as "I want to earn 50 percent more money this year than I did last year," or internal, such as "I want to be more assertive with my family." Internal goals usually refer to behavioral, cognitive,

or emotional patterns that you want to change. Business management guru Peter F. Drucker developed the acronym S.M.A.R.T. for effective goal setting. It stands for goals that are **S**pecific, **M**easurable, **A**ction-Oriented, **R**ealistic, and **T**ime-based. You can adapt Drucker's system to guide you in your personal change efforts.

Specific goals are precise. "Saving five thousand dollars by December 1" is preferable to "putting some money away for the holidays." Goals should be **Measurable** because you need to know definitively when you have accomplished what you set out to do. For personal change processes, **Action-oriented** goals are best. Actions in this context are things that you do that others can see. They are behaviors. What do you want to do more or less? Remember that you have the most control over your own behavioral choices (see *Understand the control problem*, page 18). "Reduce the number of cigarettes I smoke from two packs a day to one by January 1" is a specific, action-oriented commitment. Goals that target distorted thinking patterns might start like this: "I would like to be a less pessimistic person." Make this an action-oriented goal by rephrasing it to "I will choose to have negative thoughts without accepting them as facts. I will enlist the help of my best friend to see if she notices a change in my demeanor during the next four weeks." An emotional pattern goal might start as "I want to be a more joyful person," and evolve into "I will increase my opportunities for joyful feelings by doing one thing that I am passionate about each day for the next month."

Keep your goals **Realistic**. Perfectionists often fall into the trap of continually setting enormous goals for themselves and fully expecting to accomplish them. This is a setup for failure and demoralization. Remember to use your discernment skill when setting goals. You can only achieve what is in your power (see *Understand the control problem*, page 18). Finally, effective goals are **Time-based**. Setting a time by which you expect to accomplish the goal establishes accountability and increases the likelihood of effectiveness. You are far more likely to see the Eiffel Tower when your goal is to "travel to Paris in June of this year" than if it is "I hope I get to go to Paris someday."

Commit to yourself that you are going to live by them

The effectiveness of accountability in change efforts has been established through scientific research. A study published in 2003 by Steven McClaran, PhD, showed that working with a personal trainer accelerated people's progress through the stages of change faster than starting a new exercise program alone. In other words, you are more likely to go to the gym if you are paying for it and someone is waiting for you at a specific time. Similarly, research scientist Stanley Heshka, PhD, and his colleagues published a study indicating that weight loss was three times more effective for people who attended structured meetings versus those who dieted alone.

Be accountable for living your meaningful life.

Be accountable for living your meaningful life. First, establish your personal passions (see *Define your passions*, page 52). Commit to yourself that you are going to live by them, then share your commitment with at least one other person. This could be your partner, your best friend, a parent, a coach, a therapist, or all of the above. Establish accountability and your effort will be more effective.

Having goals and holding them loosely

Responding with them often

Specific—make your goal statements as detailed as possible.

Measureable—establish how you will track your progress to your goal.

Action-oriented—focus your goals on your behavior. It is within your control.

Realistic—do not set yourself up to fail with perfectionism.

Time-based—build accountability by giving yourself a deadline.

Resilience

RESILIENCE

Resilience is the ability to recover quickly from a setback, and meaningful living requires that you have it. There will be obstacles to your meaningful life within you and around you. This is expected. You will have setbacks. What matters is only how effectively you deal with them when they occur.

Listen for your mind's programming

Earlier, I used the personal computer as an analogy for thinking about your mind. Your biology is the hardware, your life experience is the software, and the important people from your life are some of your software programmers. Unlike your computer, however, your mind does not have a delete function. Sometimes, when you have an old software program on your computer, you remove it. Unfortunately, old mental programs like negative self-talk, toxic core beliefs, and outdated coping strategies cannot be put in the trash bin.

Unfortunately, old mental programs like negative self-talk, toxic core beliefs, and outdated coping strategies cannot be put in the trash bin.

Listen *for* your programming (thoughts, feelings, memories, urges, and sensations) but not *to* them. Your old programming will

You cannot completely control what things your mind retrieves

likely emerge during times of stress. This does not mean that your change process has failed. It means you are human with a human mind that recalls things. This is good that you can remember your own personal history. Unfortunately, you cannot completely control what things your mind retrieves.

For illustration, use this exercise from Acceptance and Commitment Therapy (ACT). Finish these three sentences:

Mary had a little _____.
Row, row, row your _____.
Happy Birthday to _____.

Your mind fills in the blanks automatically. Nothing could stop those thoughts because they have been imprinted in your mind by years of repetition. What programs have been imprinted on you? When they come up, try not to overrespond to them. Instead, accept them as information about how much pressure you had at that time in your life.

Products of the mind

For every action, there is an equal and opposite reaction.
—Sir Isaac Newton, *Mathematic Principles of Natural Philosophy*

A system is a group of related elements that form a complex whole. Getting to my office this morning, I dealt with my home security system, the automobile traffic regulation system, the U.S. economic system, and the office building's security system. Social systems are groups of related people that form a similarly complex whole like a government, family, or work group. While you are an integral part of social systems, you do not need anyone's consent to make changes within your own life. However, you do have to deal with resistance from those systems and the people in them.

Systems gravitate toward equilibrium. Equilibrium is the system's comfort zone where there is no stress. As you change personally, you will affect your social systems. This will inadvertently push people out of their comfort zones. Resistance will follow. Your partner, your children, your

Deal effectively with resistance

Deal effectively with resistance

parents, or your boss may encourage you to go back to the way you were living before. This is not out of spite or maliciousness. They are just members of systems that are trying to get back to equilibrium. Deal effectively with your social systems to maintain your changes toward meaningful living.

As you change personally, you will affect your social systems. This will inadvertently push people out of their comfort zones. Resistance will follow.

Families are examples of social systems that can resist change. Have you ever noticed that when you spend time around your parents or siblings that the old family system takes over? It doesn't matter how old you are, the system pulls you into old roles. You will always be a son or a daughter, but systemic roles like "little sister," "big brother," "baby of the family," or "the only

Within your own life

child" inevitably start to emerge. One minute you are a mature adult, and the next, you are arguing with your siblings just like when you were a kid. Sibling rivalries resurface, or maybe you lapse back into over-functioning for a chronically needy parent. Inevitably, the family system pushes you to abandon some of your individual adult traits to appease the systemic "rules of the house." Fighting them causes new tension and stress.

Effective systemic change occurs with optimal stress that requires a balance of change and validation strategies. All the work you have done to this point in *The Art of Meaningful Living* has involved change strategies. Validation is effectively giving another person the experience of being understood and valued. Effective validation also helps other people understand that their ideas and opinions are understandable in a given situation. However, validation does not necessarily mean agreement. You can help to validate others by listening without judgment, mirroring what others communicate, recognizing and voicing the emotional states of others, and connecting other similar emotional experiences to what you witness in others.

Pushing change strategies too lightly is ineffective because the system players might still be in their comfort zones. Pushing too much change too fast within your social

Validate their experiences

systems, however, may shove others too far out of their comfort zones, triggering panic and paralysis. When paralyzed, people cannot move out of their old positions. Use validation strategies, soothe others, and guard against their panic. These skills will make the transition to the new systemic equilibrium easier. There will be initial resistance, but after the people in your social systems realize that you are not going back to the old way, the system itself will begin to change.

Your systems' initial responses to your changes might be painful to experience. Some of your friends, family, classmates, or co-workers may feel confused, angry, or betrayed when you interact with them in new ways. When this happens, validate their experiences. Seek to understand their experiences while holding firm to the changes that are important for your meaningful life. Some systems are so entrenched that change comes painfully slow. Others may not be a good fit for you. This is a difficult and often painful realization.

Grief is inevitable if you choose to leave a social system, because you are experiencing a loss. Grief is one of the painful emotional experiences that we often attempt to avoid, but as mentioned earlier, emotional avoidance moves you away from meaningful living. Like change, grief is a process. When you have something to grieve, grieve it fully, then resume your meaningful life (see *Have all of your experiences*, page 70).

Idiosyncratic aspects

Listen to others' descriptions of their experiences without judgment.

Mirror what you hear other people telling you through their verbal and nonverbal communication.

Recognize the emotional states of others and give voice to them.

Connect with other people's emotional responses by voicing what most other people would feel in the same situation.

Relate your own similar emotional experiences to their current experiences.

"WHEN YOU GET A FLAT TIRE, DON'T SLASH THE OTHER THREE"

When unexpected obstacles occur in your life that are beyond your control, be wary of your first emotional reactions. Pause and reflect on them before you act (see *Reflect on your mind*, page 24). Actions driven solely by your emotional mind can compound your problems.

Work was vital to my client Jack's meaningful life. He had set a goal to be at his desk at 7:45 a.m. five days per week. Unfortunately, one Tuesday, he woke up forty-five minutes late. This was Jack's flat tire. Jack's mind thought, "I have already missed my goal of getting to work on time, so why bother?" And he bought it. Disappointed, embarrassed, and angry with himself, Jack decided to stay in bed all day rather than face his boss. Jack's boss likely would have been disappointed with Jack's behavior if he was forty-five minutes late, but he was definitely furious about his absence. These kinds of choices were putting Jack's job in jeopardy.

Some obstacles come from within you. Under- and overexpectations of control and distorted judgments are other examples of obstacles from within you. (see *Understand the control problem*, page 18). Acting on those faulty assumptions will compound your problems. Settling for an unhealthy relationship might be a mistake, but staying in it due to the belief that "I cannot be alone" is making it worse.

Build your resilience by becoming aware of the obstacles you have and your responses to them.

What obstacles do you have in your life?

Are your responses making the problems better or worse?

What can you do differently next time?

When you make a mistake on the way to your meaningful life, don't make it worse by compounding the problem. Make an adjustment and keep going.

It's fine to get a flat tire. They are an inevitable part of life. But when you get a flat tire, you change it and keep motoring

Moving toward the destination – A & B

down the road. You don't slash the other three. When you make a mistake on the way to your meaningful life, don't make it worse by compounding the problem. Make an adjustment and keep going. Maybe you start out believing that work is the most valuable element of your meaningful life, but you discover, after experience, that friendships actually bring you the most joy. Treat this mistake as you would a flat tire. Change it by adjusting how you spend your time, and keep going.

Change is moving toward your meaningful life

Having goals related to your areas of passionate living will help you build your meaningful life, and accountability is essential to ensuring your progress. However, excessive guilt over not reaching a goal only gets in the way. Instead, have goals and hold them loosely.

Each goal has an explicit and implicit purpose. The explicit purpose is to achieve the outcome listed in the goal statement. The implicit purpose of any goal is to learn. The implicit purpose of learning allows you to succeed even when you don't meet the explicit goal statement. This prevents guilt from becoming overwhelming. An unmet goal may teach you that you set an unrealistic goal initially.

An unmet goal may teach you that you set an unrealistic goal initially.

Having goals and holding them loosely

Learn from every goal

My client Ashley's most important element of meaningful living was befriend, so she constructed a series of goals around having more contact with her friends (see *Define your passions*, page 52). Initially, she was excited about the plan, but felt dejected when she came for her follow-up session two weeks later. She had not met any of her goals in this area. She felt extremely guilty and wanted to give up on the whole idea. With a gentle reminder that the implicit idea of the exercise was to learn, we reevaluated her results. She had actually called the two people she targeted. When she could only reach them via voice mail, she called two more

Learning opportunities

people. These friends were pleased to hear from her but were too busy with their jobs to get together at that time. Ashley and I learned that she had good connections with these people and that her explicit goal statement was out of her control (see *Understand the control problem*, page 18). With a slight revision, she developed a goal statement that focused only on her efforts to contact eight people, and this time, she was successful.

Holding goals lightly with the implicit goal of learning allows you to be accountable but not overwhelmed when the explicit goal is not met. Apply this to your goal-setting exercises so that the risk of emotional pain does not cause you to avoid goal-setting altogether. Analyze the situation and learn from it. Be curious next time you do not meet a goal. The information you discover will be valuable as you set up your next set of goals or weekly tasks. Use unmet goals as learning opportunities rather than an excuse to beat yourself up or to give up on your dream altogether.

Analyze the results of unmet goals by asking:

What internal obstacles prevented you from reaching your goal?

What external obstacles prevented you from reaching your goal?

Can you eliminate these obstacles or their impact?

Was the timeframe of the goal unrealistic?

Was the explicit goal outcome completely within your control?

Is it possible that the explicit goal outcome is not a priority for you?

Make new mistakes

We all make mistakes. They are part of the human experience. The question is not whether you will make mistakes but rather, what is your relationship with those mistakes? Can you see mistakes as effective teachers, or are they shameful blunders to you? This mind monitoring exercise can help you become aware of your relationship to mistakes.

Bring your focus to a memory of a recent mistake you have made, and gently hold it. Notice your thoughts, feelings, sensations, and urges as you hold the memory in your mind.

What came to your mind? Whatever the answer, do not judge yourself. Simply notice what your mind generated. Learning from your mistakes is congruent with meaningful living while avoid-

Do not beat yourself up

ing them is a path to avoidant living (see *Choose your style of living*, page 10).

Learning from your mistakes is congruent with meaningful living while avoiding them is a path to avoidant living.

Once you establish a helpful relationship with your mistakes, commit to making new ones. Building your meaningful life by making the same mistakes over and over is like trying to learn mathematics by solving "2 + 2" over and over. To be successful in either circumstance, you will need to learn more.

My client, Joan, built her meaningful life around her passion of partnering. Her intimate relationship with her husband was one of her top priorities, and Joan was trying desperately to get along with her mother-in-law. Unfortunately, they fought often. Joan's strategy for reducing the fighting was to be nicer to her husband's mom. It never worked. No matter how nice Joan was, her mother-in-law became angry eventually. The strategy was a mistake, and Joan kept making it. As we talked about the situation, it became clear that her mother-in-law had an assertive personality and did not respect

Making the same mistakes over and over is like trying to learn mathematics

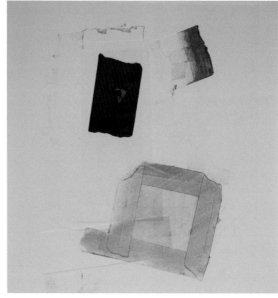

Make purposeful choices

people who behaved differently. Together, Joan and I came up with strategies that she could use to set limits and boundaries with her mother-in-law. It was important for Joan to be respectful, and we found strategies that were mannerly but firm. As Joan tried her new strategy, she got different results. It seemed that the fighting with her mother-in-law decreased but did not stop. We discussed the new situation. It appeared that the new strategies did not work when her mother-in-law drank alcohol. When drinking, it was only a matter of time until the mother-in-law's anger boiled over onto everyone around her. We hypothesized that the alcohol lowered her inhibitions, and anger came through that had nothing to do with Joan. Thus, we developed a plan for Joan to limit the amount of time that she spent around her mother-in-law at occasions where alcohol was served. The combination of these new strategies was effective for her and ultimately helpful for her marriage.

What mistakes do you keep repeating? Identify them, and then try a new strategy. Anything new will give you new information. Consider the data and make adjustments. Since you are going to make mistakes anyway, make new ones.

Accept them as information about how much pressure you had

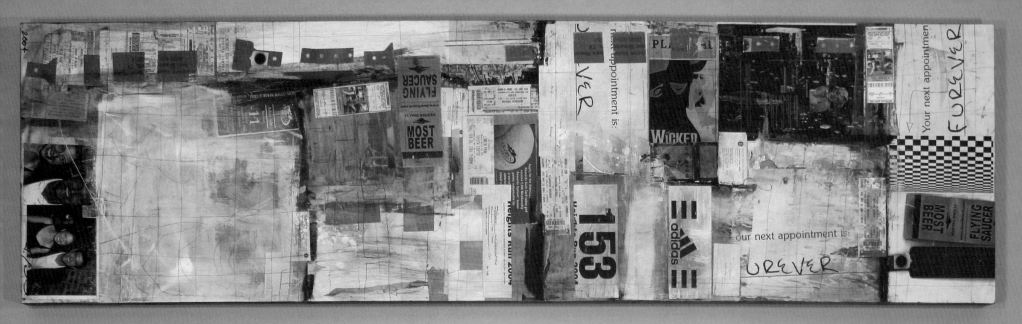

The Art of
Meaningful Lives

The following ten people are truly living their meaningful lives, proof that meaningful living is possible for each of us. Their unique elements of meaningful living have been captured in words and art. The biographies accompanying each profile were partially inspired by Andy Warhol's iconic portraiture pieces from the 1960s, '70s, and '80s. The biographies reveal the story within each individual's meaningful life. Artist John Palmer says, "The most important part of creating a collage biography is discovering the person I'm working with. My goal is to assemble a completely meaningful portrait of what is uniquely valuable to them." The collage biographies are as unique as the lives they depict. Some are single pieces and others are a three-piece set, representing different phases of a career or relationship. It is my sincere hope that, like these people, you find your passions and live them.

Our story (triptych)

Mr. Bob Devlin

Vice President, General Manager
Neiman Marcus Group Inc.

Having spent his entire career with Neiman Marcus, work is vital to Mr. Devlin's meaningful life. Those who know him describe him as dedicated and disciplined with remarkable focus and attention to detail.

Mr. Devlin also makes serving others part of his meaningful life by volunteering his time and energy to Houston, Texas, area organizations like the Houston Ballet, Child Advocates, and the Houston Grand Opera.

Dr. Carolyn Farb, hc

Philanthropist

Carolyn Farb's meaningful life exemplifies element of service. The native Texan serves on numerous boards including serving as the Chairman of the Board for UNICEF, the HuffIngton Center on Aging, The Texas Innocence Network, Children of Nicaragua Rotarian Project and Rotarian International Efforts. Farb's most recent honors include the President's Volunteer Service Award, the Diana Award, and YWCA Woman of the Year. Dr. Farb was a Community Hero Torchbearer for the 1996 Olympics and is a recipient of the Children"s Medallion of Honor from UNICEF. Dr. Farb is a member of the Texas Philanthropy Hall of Fame.

Mr. Donn Fullenweider

Attorney at Law, Founder
The Fullenweider Firm

A man of style and substance, Mr. Fullenweider embraces the elements of work, nurture, and play in his daily life. Mr. Fullenweider's career in family law has brought him great success and acclaim. He is literally a living legend, as recognized in the Hall of Legends of the State Bar of Texas, and is also a diplomat in the American College of Family Trial Lawyers.

Mr. Fullenweider lives the element of nurturing by being an active part of his family with his wife, son, stepson, and three grandchildren. Play is also part of Mr. Fullenweider's meaningful life, as he is an avid skier, sailor, and abstract artist. Those who know him describe him as a trustworthy, ethical, and charismatic man who is a stable force that enhances the lives of those connected to him.

Ms. Joanne King Herring

Political Activist, Humanitarian

No one embodies service with style and grace quite like Ms. Herring. She has been named the Cultural Leader of the Year and one of the Ten Most Legendary Women in the United States. She is a winner of the Sitara Medal and has been Honorary Consul to the Kingdom of Morocco and the Republic of Pakistan.

Ms. Herring nurtures her two sons and has an active spiritual life that allows her to transcend cultural barriers in the United States and beyond. Academy Award-winning actress Julia Roberts depicted Ms. Herring's meaningful life in the 2007 feature film, *Charlie Wilson's War.*

Ms. Charlotte Landram

Author, Speaker

Ms. Landrum combines the elements of work and growth into her career as a personal coach. Some have called Ms. Landrum a "white light" who is committed to nurturing others in her practice as a coach. She provides her clients and those around her with profound insights. She believes in working through issues with her clients.

Mr. Carl Lewis

World-Class Athlete, Actor

Mr. Fredrick Carlton Lewis is an international celebrity, given his work as a track and field athlete. The ten-time Olympic medalist and the 1980s' Athlete of the Decade believes we all should "experience life to the fullest, reinvent ourselves…and go for it again." This captures Mr. Lewis's belief in personal growth.

Mr. Lewis's meaningful life would not be possible without his family of origin. Born to athletic and activist parents in Birmingham, Alabama, Mr. Lewis is one of four siblings. He credits his father's dedication to the American civil rights movement as one of the inspirations for his success.

Mr. Taft McWhorter and Mrs. Dana McWhorter

Partners

Partnering is vital to this couple's meaningful life together. Taft and Dana McWhorter have been married for nineteen years and have three sons, Andrew, Zachary, and Taylor. Their family life is focused on a deep, mutual respect for each other and their individual passions.

Mr. McWhorter is a dreamer and a visionary person. As business manager of John Palmer Art, he embodies the entrepreneurial spirit that so often shows in those whose meaningful lives are enriched by work.

Mrs. McWhorter is a nurturer. She has lived her passion for loving and caring for children with her family and her work in the library at an elementary school.

Mr. Robert Rauschenberg

Artist, American Icon

A titan of the world art scene for six decades, Mr. Robert Rauschenberg embodied growth in his meaningful life. He once said, "I usually work in a direction until I know how to do it, then I stop. At the time I am bored or understand—I use those words interchangeably—another appetite has formed." His passion for growth in his art and in his life made him arguably the most important American artist of the twentieth century. Mr. Rauschenberg also transcended the monotony of everyday things by finding beauty in them and incorporating them into his art. A blanket, a fork, a tire track were never more beautiful as when they were used in one of Mr. Rauschenberg's masterpieces.

Mr. Dominic Walsh

Dancer, Founder
Dominic Walsh Dance Theater

Mr. Walsh's work is art, and he has built Dominic Walsh Dance Theater, founded in 2002. The Houston, Texas, contemporary dance company has received critical acclaim from publications like *Dance Magazine*, the *Houston Chronicle*, and *Dance International Magazine*. Mr. Walsh's dedication, innovation, and high standards of performance attract some of the world's most promising artists to the company. Mr. Walsh transcends the conventional boundaries and limitations of ballet performance. As he says, "This ain't *Swan Lake*."

Live your meaningful life

How do you envision your meaningful life as art? What are the stories of your past that form your personal biography? What experiences do you want to add to your life story? Perhaps you imagine a depiction of a romantic partnership, your family of origin, your career, or your friends—the family of your choosing. Try not to judge what your mind gives you. Rather, accept the results as information pointing you toward what is uniquely meaningful to you. This image is the vision of your meaningful life. Make your vision reality by using the concepts, skills, and anecdotes from this book in your life today. Thank you for your time, your openness, and your courage as you being to live more passionately. I wish you all the best.

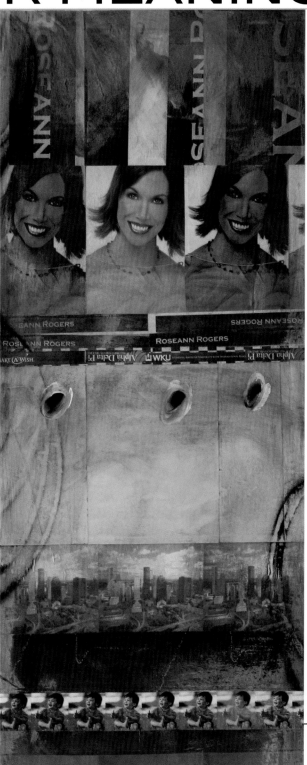

Roseann Rogers - biography

Christopher F. Brown, LCSW, MBA

Christopher F. Brown is a native Louisianan and adopted Texan working in private practice as a psychotherapist in the Houston, Texas, area. Christopher answered a calling to enter the helping profession of clinical social work after spending six years working as a human resources director and operations manager for his third-generation family business.

Christopher believes that each person is wonderfully unique and that any helping process should begin in a respectful and nonjudgmental fashion. To Christopher, psychotherapy and coaching are collaborative processes whose outcomes are ultimately driven by his clients. With this belief, it is fitting that Christopher's first book, *The Art of Meaningful Living*, is a collaboration with artist John Palmer.

"There is no simple answer," says Brown to the existential pain that he sees in his office on a daily basis, but "hope is essential. I have hope and the deep belief that we can all find meaning in our lives every day." In his work, Christopher starts where his clients are in their lives, and he partners with them to reach their goals.

About the Author and Artist

Christopher has himself embraced the art of meaningful living. Every day he strives to do something that strengthens his partnership with his wife, Melissa. He tries to take care of himself mentally and physically, and plays every chance he gets.

John Palmer

John Palmer's art and his path are free, full of light, and alive with energy and movement. From all of his creations, the collector can discern a two- or three-dimensional extension of Palmer's personality. The moment someone takes a step into Palmer's chic gallery and studio, he or she enters a fresh, vibrant universe.

An artist, however talented, requires knowledge of technique as a means of harnessing that talent. Palmer has honed his distinctive technique through his love of travel, with art exploration and study in all corners of the world, including Barcelona, Buenos Aires, Montreal, Florence, Athens, Tokyo, Mexico, Cape Town, and Paris. Palmer's most renowned experience in this vein was studying in Florence, Italy, at the Santa Reparata International School of Art.

Palmer is always on the cusp of a new adventure. His current projects include a new series entitled "Notable Biographies," featuring Palmer's collage style. Each biography is a one-of-a-kind piece of fine artwork that incorporates the personal effects and memorabilia of its collector, creating an irreplaceable patchwork of his or her life.

Palmer believes that education, combined with hard work, is the key to his success and artistic evolution. He is now represented in galleries across the United States and abroad.

Palmer has only just launched his artistic and emotional course. The journey is certain to be vibrant, exciting, and full of energy…very much like the artist himself.

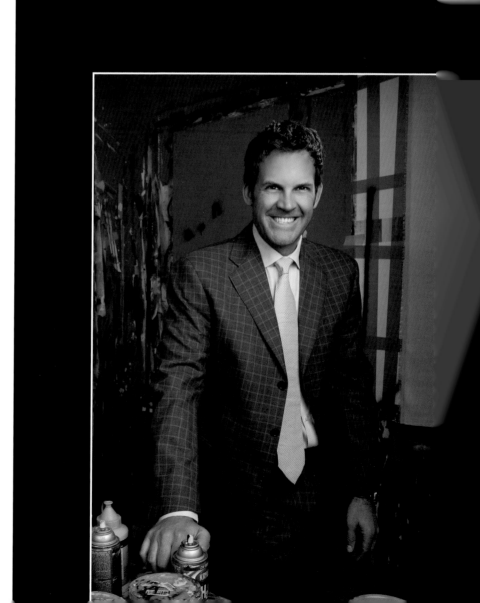

Acknowledgments

My sincere thanks to Melissa Martinez, my wife, who loves me, supports me, and always tells me like it is; we did it. To John Palmer, my friend, without whose talent and energy this book would never have happened; to Sharron Mapel who helped me find the courage to see this through; to John Hill, my brother, Kimberly Noble, my sister, and Amanda Lewis, my friend, who volunteered to be my first editors at the very reasonable fee of nothing; to Amanda Assali and the rest of the lovely people with John Palmer Art, who are always a joy to work with; and to the staffs at Synergy Books and Phenix & Phenix Literary Publicists, who were willing to take a chance on this project.

Thank you to the collectors of John Palmer's art who allowed their pieces to be featured in this book: Carolyn Farb, hc, Nico and Erica Sprotti, Dick Tate, Robin Palmer and Joan Taliaferro, Ted Holubec and Allie Levy, and Debra Hymel Levy.

To my clients past and present, I am humbled by what you are willing to share of yourselves with me. I am more for having known each of you. You have my most heartfelt support and gratitude.

Catalysts I

Finally, I want to acknowledge my mom, Natalee Frier Farasey, who introduced John Palmer and me, and John's dad, Clifford E. Palmer. These two people, who are no longer with us in body, influenced every page of this book.

John started painting in 1998 as a way to deal with his grief over the death of his father. He did not know how much this coping strategy would change his life. From making his first five pieces in 1998, his career change to artist, his first show in 1999, to today, John's success has been a boon for his staff, his collectors, and himself.

As for Mom, she taught me how to carry myself by the way she carried herself—with style and grace; she infused me with me with her love for design and art (especially anything by Robert Rauschenberg); and she always said I would write a book. She was right. I began writing *The Art of Meaningful Living* after my mom died in 2006.

Mom, it's not the story of Julia the chicken, but here it is. I miss you every day.

—Christopher F. Brown

Catalysts II